# Closing Arguments
## The Last Battle

**Fredric G. Levin**
**Mike Papantonio**
**Martin Levin**

A SEVILLE SQUARE BOOK
Pensacola, Florida

FIRST EDITION

**A Seville Square Book**
FIRST EDITION

**Seville Publishing**
*Correspondence:*
Post Office Box 12042
Pensacola, FL 32590

*Office:*
316 South Baylen
Fourth Floor
Pensacola, FL 32501
(850) 435-7165

www.sevillepublishing.com

**Closing Arguments**
*The Last Battle*
Seville Square, First Edition, April 2003
Cover Design: Susan Rand www.duncanmccall.com

**ISBN 0-9649711-3-5**

# ABOUT THE COVER

In 1878 Carl Haag discovered the substance and heart of a true warrior through the image of a Viking chieftain. We do not need an art critic or a historian to tell us that Haag distinctively captured the critically important qualities of a warrior.

The authors chose Haag's masterpiece for the cover of this book because we believe trial lawyers will benefit by taking the time to analyze what Haag's painting expresses in regard to the perfect warrior.

There are many dimensions to the character Haag portrays as best equipped to consistently succeed in battle. If you look closely, Haag did not paint the eyes of a shallow, dull-minded, hulking barbarian. In fact, the eyes Haag chose easily could have been those of a philosopher, a poet, a scientist, a teacher, or a writer. They are eyes that, in the heat of battle, can look threatening but nonetheless are filled with something that looks like understanding, wisdom, compassion, empathy, and keen worldly insight.

This perfect warrior that Haag created in hundreds of shades of watercolors carries the war axe of a chieftain. It is an axe that he knows how to use and is not afraid to use. But chances are he knows when to lay it down and choose a better weapon, or possibly even another day and place to fight.

Finally, this perfect warrior has the weathered visage of an individual who has endured through the continued agony of losses and ecstasy of victories. Yet, no matter how worn he has and will become, he recognizes and accepts his responsibility to wake up each day prepared and willing to once again fight.

We are proud to state that this painting hung in our law offices for twenty-five years. Each day lawyers would find a new quality or nuance about the painting that they had not noticed the day before. What the lawyers finally concluded is that while Haag's painting is that of a Viking warrior, it just as easily could have been that of a trial lawyer.

*The authors wish to thank Allen and Teri Levin for the use of their painting.*

# TABLE OF CONTENTS

## INTRODUCTION

We have all read trial advocacy books covering "the art" of opening statement, direct examination, cross-examination, and even closing argument. Most often, these books have been written by attorneys who have had little or no real trial experience. Instead, they speak from the experience of others or from the perspective of a hypothetical vacuum.

The arguments and issues presented in this book have been confronted by the authors individually and collectively throughout their careers as trial lawyers. The suggested recommendations are not in the nature of a theoretical discussion about what might or might not work in a "perfect world" trial setting. They represent the best of what three trial lawyers have learned in more than seventy collective years of incredibly rewarding victories and agonizing defeats.

This is not a book of war stories designed to suggest that the authors have command of some unique skill that exceeds the potential skill of any trial lawyer reading this book. It is merely a road map that discusses places where these authors have made a few correct turns and where they have completely run off the road in their efforts to learn the mysterious art of courtroom trial advocacy.

This book has been organized in a way that will allow you to proceed quickly to a specific page and find ideas and sometimes complete answers about problems that predictably arise in most trials.

Obviously, the collection of arguments covered in this book is not exhaustive because every trial brings its unique collection of problems. In fact, it is the unpredictable element of jury trials that keeps our job as trial lawyers exciting and often downright terrifying. But then again, trial law never has been and never will be for the faint at heart.

Instead, trial law is for the warrior who continues to prepare for and fight a battle every day. It is for the warrior who marches forward with precision and direction, despite defeats and despite criticism from those who watch from the sidelines, pretending to be the champion of the world yet never entering the ring.

# Chapter 1
# THE FUNDAMENTALS OF A CLOSING ARGUMENT

### *The Importance of the Closing*

How important is closing argument to the outcome of a trial? There have been many studies by psychologists, attorneys, and jury research professionals in regard to the scientific answer to this question, and of course, the conclusions vary from extreme importance to little importance. We submit that the best way to answer this question is to assume that the plaintiff's counsel stands in front of the jury in summation and states that the defendant was 100 percent liable for the collision and that the plaintiff's damages total $1,500,000. Counsel for the defendant refuses to make a closing argument. What is the jury likely to do? Similarly, assume that plaintiff's counsel makes an outstanding summation and defense counsel presents an ineffective, poorly planned, and inarticulate closing. What is the jury likely to do?

As significant as opening statement is to the successful presentation of a trial, one attorney may waive or defer his opening statement or make a horrible opening statement and yet win the case through the introduction of his evidence and an effective closing argument. Similarly, we have all stood in a courtroom where our cases have dismantled before our eyes as we have watched witnesses on cross and even witnesses on our direct do their very best to burn our cases to the ground. Yet we still won those cases through an effective closing argument. But one thing is certain: if a lawyer's closing argument is poorly presented, there is no other opportunity for the attorney to salvage his case.

We have all read or heard about jury research which concludes that 80 percent of the jurors reach their ultimate conclusion as to who should win after opening statements. The authors' experience does not corroborate this highly suspect statistic. The opening statement is obviously extremely important because it provides you the opportunity to summarize the evidence and establish the theme of the trial prior to the presentation of the testimony. Without an effective opening statement, it may be very difficult for the jury to understand the presentation of evidence in a complicated case, and you could lose the case long before you get to your closing statement.

On the other hand, we believe that very few jurors develop an opinion that is fixed in concrete after only hearing an opening statement. While many jurors may take a position after opening statements, in most cases it is a position that is constantly changing and being developed as events in the trial unfold. More than a few contemporary studies have demonstrated that witness testimony and closing statements have the most impact on a juror's final determination. Juror studies also show that most jurors actually try to heed the judge's caution to refrain from finding for one side or another until all the witnesses, evidence, and arguments have been presented.

Unlike the opening statement, the closing argument provides you the opportunity to speak directly with the jurors. It provides you a time to explain the validity of your evidence and argue the justness of your case. While juries are primarily dependent upon the evidence presented during trial, empirical research demonstrates that jurors recall portions of the opening and closing better than any other portion of the trial. Much of the trial testimony becomes jumbled in the minds of many jurors. Very few cases are clear-cut based solely on the evidence presented. In most cases, the majority of the evidentiary proceedings have a tendency to be overly meticulous, boring, and confusing to the typical juror. This is caused in part by our evidentiary rules and trial procedures. However, when you add to the scenario a minimally talented trial judge and a poorly thought-out evidence and testimony presentation, the problem increases exponentially. In the end, it becomes very difficult for juries to put the evidence in perspective without the benefit of a powerful and concise opening statement and closing argument.

Many of us have read the outstanding closing arguments delivered by the great pioneers of trial advocacy. Even if we had the ability to deliver these closings, it is doubtful that such grandiose summations would be effective in this day and time. There are many reasons for this. Jury cynicism is at an all-time high. Some of the heartstring tugs that were routinely made a part of closing arguments thirty years ago are more often regarded as suspect, manipulative, and insincere when delivered in courtrooms today. However, with this said, our experience shows that the closing argument is probably more important today than it has been in years past.

### Purpose of Closing Argument

The purpose of closing argument is to summarize the evidence presented and argue the conclusions to be drawn from the evidence. The closing argument is the final opportunity a lawyer has to speak with the jury about the evidence and the law. The sole purpose of the attorney's closing argument is to concisely and briefly incorporate all positive and negative evidence into one theme in such a way that the evidence presented is consistent with the attorney's themes and theory of the case. It is the time when the attorney points to and leads the jury to a place where the jury can naturally, logically, instinctively, judgmentally, emotionally conclude that the intelligent, fair, just, politically correct, legally correct, morally correct thing to do is to find for that attorney's client. By doing this effectively in the opening portion of the closing argument, you will limit the ability of the opposing counsel to respond. More importantly, the purpose of closing argument is to provide ammunition to those members of the jury who want to argue on behalf of your client in the jury room. Your words, ideas, and conviction arm your juror allies for the fight back in the jury room.

### When to Prepare Closing Argument

Prepare a first-draft closing statement at the beginning of your trial preparation process before your preparation of the voir dire, direct and cross-examinations, and opening statement. You should do this in order to better understand the key points and themes to be presented at trial. What you put on paper in that first draft will take the shape of a North Star that will lead the direction and focus of your entire trial presentation. Those early drafts of your "wish list closing argument" will become the road map that will help you lead a jury to where you want to take them. By constantly focusing on that planned closing argument, you increase the likelihood that all important aspects of your voir dire, opening statement, evidence, and witness testimony will be consistently and insightfully presented during trial, without conflicting, confusing, and disjointed evidence being introduced. Of course, you will be continuously revising your closing argument during trial in order to address all positive and negative points that become an issue.

### The Length of Your Closing Argument

During a trial, jurors have the difficult task of processing significant amounts of information, often with conflicting content acquired over a prolonged period of time. Consequently, in close cases, many extraneous influences intervene in the jury's final decision. Moreover, there are significant individual differences in jurors' ability to maintain interest and concentration over a period of time. Individual variables such as susceptibility to distraction and fatigue, age, intelligence, physical disabilities, and boredom all impact on how much of an attorney's presentation a juror comprehends or retains.

The nature and format of the closing argument has by necessity changed significantly over the last few decades. Our culture has helped develop an overwhelming majority of people with an extremely short attention span. We process information in "sound bites" and by reading headlines. We learn more from what we see because of our exposure to television shows, motion pictures, and high-tech computer presentations. While the human intellect is remarkable, it has limitations, particularly in retaining all the details that may be introduced at trial. Jurors are used to seeing and hearing Hollywood-quality five-minute summations on television lawyer shows.

What a juror comprehends and remembers is overwhelmingly subjective and not easily predictable. It occurs in a sometimes wildly random manner and differs from juror to juror. Accordingly, trial attorneys must find a way to simplify their presentation and closing argument, and present a fast-paced, stimulating case. Some of the largest verdicts in the country have occurred in trials of three days or less, and with closing arguments not exceeding thirty minutes.

The attorney must control the presentation of the trial and certainly the closing by painstakingly evaluating and reevaluating the case. Success lies in selecting only a few key issues and then making certain those issues presented are the most pertinent and clear-cut when the last words are spoken during closing. In fact, an attorney must often forgo introducing possibly helpful evidence because it will unnecessarily delay and often complicate the presentation of trial. This type of lawyering sometimes requires a huge amount of discipline because it is contrary to our nature. We often are so close to the minutiae and details of a case that we want to show off our command of the facts. In closing arguments, we too often want to let the jury know that we have worked hard in preparing our case and that nothing has gotten by us. We too often want to leave the jury with the impression that we are the grand master of every detail that they have been exposed to in the course of the trial, and therefore, we certainly should be entitled to a favorable verdict. The bad news is that most experienced trial lawyers will tell you it doesn't work that way.

Will Rogers had it right when he said; "I never heard a good long speech nor a bad short speech." This also applies to closing arguments, especially after a long trial. The shorter, more concise, and structured the closing argument, the more effective it will be.

## Chapter 2
## DEVELOPING A THEME FOR CLOSING ARGUMENT

### *Power of Theme*

Most trial attorneys are bound and determined to control, direct, and fashion almost every aspect of their lives. Their desire to be in control sometimes pushes them toward controlling the facts of their case in the way they would prefer the facts to be rather than the way they really find them. They are slow to catch onto the idea that: "If it doesn't fit, then don't force it."

The better trial lawyers at some point in their career have learned that you engineer the themes of your case around the facts that you have been dealt–warts and all. In fact, these lawyers are wise enough to understand that when they become insightful and creative with the facts they have been dealt, their case begins to look better than the improbable, inconsistent, unlikely case they might create by wandering too far away from the truth.

There are many reasons that classic historical novels and well-written biographies about sometimes boring people sell as well as they do. At least one reason is that a good historical writer or a good biographer takes the worst of the facts, the least interesting facts, the most tedious facts, the facts that he wishes he could change, and skillfully creates an entertaining story that can stand the scrutiny of a million readers. The job of a trial lawyer requires that same skill.

If we had at our fingertips a collection of the very best speeches and arguments ever written by the world's greatest orators, we would probably see a pattern of similarity take shape. A major part of that similarity would be that those speeches and arguments rely heavily on timeless themes. They are themes that mankind has grown up with—themes that help mankind grow. The essence of those themes has been extracted from mankind's greatest religions. They have been extracted from our classic literature, our philosophy, our poetry, and our art. They are truths that, when spoken, provide us comfort, courage, motivation, and inspiration. When we hear these themes laid out for us, they remind us of the wisdom in being more compassionate, more open-minded, less prejudiced, more forgiving, more decent. The successful trial lawyer must learn to tap into that same wisdom when arguing to a jury. The trial lawyer must find his "best self" in order to receive a fair and just verdict in his case.

Clarence Darrow never delivered a closing argument that did not borrow the very best of these types of timeless themes. When Darrow stood up in front of a jury to deliver his closing statement, he would extend his arms from his six-foot frame and embrace the jury with the wisdom he had learned from Solomon, Socrates, Plato, Aristotle, Homer, Dante, Martin Luther, Shakespeare, Da Vinci, and most every great thinker who had gone before him.

The world's great orators have always had the ability to weave larger-than-life themes into their spoken word in such a way that their effort is hardly noticeable; their theme is effectively repackaged, and their message invites us to be our best selves. We have heard more than a few truly great trial lawyers state that too many younger trial lawyers are too many parts technician and too few parts philosopher, classical thinker, artist, and creative dreamer.

The top ten percent of most law school graduates can tell a judge everything he might want to know about Judge Cardozo's opinion in *Palsgraf v. Long Island R.R. Co.* Yet at the same time, most of them are woefully unequipped to move a jury with the timeless ideas of

10

Shakespeare. Playing the role of technician or thinking like a lawyer is the easy portion of a great argument. It is playing the role of artist, creative thinker, philosopher, theologian, statesman, and poet that requires the hard work. It is this type of work that we cannot cram into our lives two weeks before we are supposed to deliver our most important closing argument. Instead, we need to make it a part of our lives every day. It is the type of work we must begin years before we are ever asked to walk into a courtroom and deliver the most important argument in our career.

In spite of what we would like to believe, "thinking like a lawyer" is really not that difficult. After all, it is merely a way of thinking that has been handed down to us from preceding generations of lawyers. We are kidding ourselves if we believe that we own any high ground in the world of great ideas and wisdom simply because we have been trained to "think like a lawyer." For the most part, jurors are absolutely unimpressed with our training and ability to "think like a lawyer" in closing argument. Most of the time, it is common sense and passion that move a jury in a close call. Common sense and passion are often missing in the "technician's" closing argument as he thinks like a lawyer while the jurors are thinking about their life experiences.

Flannery O'Conner will probably always be regarded as one of America's great short story writers. She had one easily identifiable quality about her writing that she shared with all the Conrads, the Hemingways, the Salingers, and the Fitzgeralds of this world. That quality is that she mastered the use of themes. Her short stories worked a single theme to the edge of exhaustion without ever getting close to exhausting the reader. Her stories were rich with themes about values, racial bias, greed, lust, sloth, and hope in the "New South," and she delivered those themes while she entertained her readers.

That seems like a fairly common sense goal for any trial lawyer, but the art of theme development has received far less emphasis in an age

11

of trial laptops, PowerPoint extravaganzas, and audio and visual gadgets of almost every description. Our ability to master creative, entertaining theme development is atrophying, and our reliance on high-tech sideshows is becoming a crutch for some of us in the course of trial presentation. High-tech can be outstanding when we remember why we are using it. It can be a great tool when we remember that it is being used to emphasize and reemphasize, invent and reinvent, and create and recreate those basic, relevant themes that can be reduced to a pen-and-paper paragraph of only a few sentences.

### *A Theme Is More Than Just Words*

There are many nuances to theme development. Theme is found in more than the words you speak to a jury. It must be developed by your actions, your mannerisms, your dress, and your non-spoken image at trial. If part of your theme is that influence, power, and money are what drives the decision making of your opponent, then you must draw a clear distinction between your client and your opponent. If your theme centers around something as basic as David meets Goliath, then you and your client must project the image of an underdog shepherd boy rather than that of an arrogant, overconfident, immensely powerful giant.

It is unusual to find trial lawyers with fighter pilot, cowboy mentalities who are willing to accept the fact that the trial is not about them. The theme that they need to be developing is not about them. They sometimes have a difficult time accepting that as the trial lawyer, they are simply the conduit for the theme. If understated humility is what is needed to project a chosen theme, then we must have the ability, discipline, and willingness to fit into that persona. Our mannerisms need to blend with the words we are using to convince the jury on our theme.

There is a well-known and well-respected trial lawyer from Georgia who is typically recruited to defend corporations who have engaged in conduct that usually makes these corporations subject to punitive damages. This defense lawyer has mastered the use of a theme that works to minimize damages no matter how reprehensible the conduct of that corporation might have been. His theme, broadly stated, is that decent employees—employees who are terrific mothers and fathers of terrific children—should not be indirectly punished because of the deplorable conduct and decision making of a greedy few. He is able to spin the image of a company that is made up of people who are just like the people sitting in the jury box. The corporations he defends in those high-risk cases are filled with decent, hardworking people who would never dream of causing harm to an American consumer.

He is not afraid to shed the image of the combative, fierce-looking warrior and project an image of the humble, reserved peacemaker who appears to be out-skilled and generally out-lawyered by his powerful opponent throughout the entire course of the trial. He has an ego that is well-adjusted enough to allow him to appear overpowered, outmaneuvered, and painfully disturbed by the conduct of those "few greedy people" who have made his multi-billion dollar corporation into a "victim"! By the end of the trial, he begins to look like his theme in every respect.

### What Does a Theme Look Like?

Developing an effective theme and selling the facts of your case to a jury has nothing in common with what a car salesman typically does when he sets out to sell a previously owned fixer-upper to a would-be buyer. Aside from the obvious fact that most used car salesmen don't fall within the category of being officers of the court, here are some other important distinctions: The car salesman during his thirty-minute exposure to his would-be buyer will likely take the path of least resistance and shade the truth about how well a transmission works or how many miles a car has traveled. His exposure to the buyer is very limited. His audience does not have the opportunity to uncover the flaws running through his facts or his character. But your audience will be listening to you, watching you, and analyzing everything about the underlying facts of your themes for days, weeks—months in a complex case. Because of that, hedging, puffing, distorting, hiding, misrepresenting, and deodorizing your facts to fit a theme has the potential to be disastrous.

As a trial lawyer, it is not your role to make all the barnacles and bad facts that you inherited simply disappear. The best closers are able to be honest with themselves in regard to the facts they have on their side. Any of us who grew up watching Popeye cartoons will remember that short, unattractive, sometimes dim-witted character declaring to the world, "I am what I am, and that's all that I am." Lawyers should show that kind of honesty when it comes to matching up the facts of their case with the theme they intend to convey to the jury. What you learned as a child about a lie is still true in our adult lives as lawyers. That is, once you start moving away from the truth, it becomes harder and harder to hold your story together. Thus, work with and stick with the truth.

In order to develop this type of theme, counsel must be thoroughly prepared for trial. He should have analyzed the strengths and weaknesses of his case (from an objective standpoint), and should have analyzed the adversary's strengths and weaknesses. Counsel must not approach trial with blind confidence; for if he does, he will tend to belittle the opposition's strongest points, and fail to compensate for the weaknesses in his own case.

A trial lawyer must be able to answer the following questions: (1) Who is the opposing counsel; and what approach has he taken in the past? (2) Does opposing counsel come across well? (3) What kind of person is the plaintiff, and what kind of impression will he make? (4) Who are plaintiff's witnesses, and are they believable? (5) Who is the opposing party, and what kind of impression will he make? (6) Who are the opposing party's witnesses, and are they believable? and (7) What are your strongest and weakest points, and what are the strongest and weakest points of your opposition? The answers to these questions will be critical in developing an effective theme.

After answering the above questions, the trial lawyer should be prepared to develop a theme (a winning strategy) for his case. To do this, he must find a reason why the jury would want to return a verdict in favor of his client. For example, such a reason could be that the client is a helpless victim, a stoic fighter, a larger-than-life father, a single-mindedly devoted, loving mother, or even an unlikable curmudgeon who is entitled to protection by the law no matter how unlikable he is. Of course, an effective theme could be based on the opposing side's horrendous conduct, attitude, and greed. Whatever theme a trial lawyer chooses, he must be sure that it is supported by the evidence and the law; and that if the jury believes the theme, then the jury will rule in favor of his client.

As an example of developing a theme, suppose you represent a plaintiff who makes a horrible witness and has contradicted himself in three different depositions. He never looks at the person with whom he is speaking, and he has absolutely no confidence in himself. Moreover, no matter how he dresses, he still gives the impression of being slovenly. A great trial lawyer must recognize and accept these facts, and attempt to work them into an effective theme. For example, if the facts support it, counsel could tell the jury about the difficulties the plaintiff had growing up; such as his inability to get dates because of his appearance. Counsel could tell about the plaintiff's inability to get a good job because he was not very intelligent, and about all the times he was kicked around when he was growing up. Counsel could state to the jury something similar to the following:

> Looking at my client sitting here today, it is easy to tell that he is scared to death. In fact, he is scared of you, the jury, he is scared of me, his own counsel, and he is most assuredly scared of Mr. Jones, counsel for the defense. In fact, my client has been so scared throughout the preparation of this trial and the actual trial, that he really does not know the true facts. He has given at least three different versions of what happened, and would likely give a fourth version if he were asked about it on the witness stand. He will simply say anything that he believes people want him to say. He will agree with whatever someone asks or tells him. For this reason, I am not going to put him on the stand and question him about liability. If the defense wishes to humiliate him, then they can call him to the stand. Fortunately in this case, we have many eyewitnesses who will tell you exactly what happened to my client. They will be the objective and disinterested voice for my client, who does not have the ability to be his own voice.

Whatever theme trial counsel chooses to present, it must be a theme that "steals the defendant's thunder." In other words, it must be a theme that incorporates all the worst evidence against your client. Counsel should keep in mind that no matter how bad the situation is, it is better for counsel to utilize it than for the other side to do so. For example, suppose you represent the plaintiff in a case, and that two police officers and three independent eyewitness will testify that the plaintiff was extremely intoxicated at one o'clock in the afternoon, and that he began staggering across a major highway when he was struck by defendant's automobile. If the facts support it, then trial counsel could present the following theme:

The plaintiff in this case, Bill Jones, is the type of person who has been working two jobs every day since his graduation from high school in order to take care of his wife and two children. On the evening before his accident, Bill did something unexpected: he came home early that evening from work to be with his wife and children. To Bill's surprise, his children were staying with the neighbor, and his wife was in bed with his best friend.

Instead of facing this problem, Bill did something he had never done: he went to a local bar and began drinking, and he continued to drink throughout the night and into the next afternoon. When Bill left the bar at one o'clock the next afternoon, Bill was as drunk as a man could possibly be and still be able to walk. He then started to cross a six-lane highway in order to get home. Bill swayed and staggered across three lanes of traffic before being hit by the defendant's vehicle.

Two police officers will say Bill's blood-alcohol level was as high as they have ever seen. Three eyewitnesses are going to say that they were driving on the highway and could clearly see that Bill had no way to protect himself because of his drunkenness, but that they had no problem avoiding him. In fact, only one person on the highway that day could not stop from hitting Bill, and that is the defendant, Sam Smith. The simple issue in this case is whether this horribly injured man should have been seen by the defendant in time for the defendant to have avoided the accident. We believe the defendant was not paying attention to his driving at the time of the accident.

The above factual scenario first appeared to be an unwinnable situation. Yet the above theme puts the defense counsel in the position of having to defend, rather than attack. It would be ridiculous for defense counsel to stand up and announce that the plaintiff was drunk, because plaintiff's counsel has already admitted that he was "as drunk as anybody could possibly be." This theme effectively "steals the defendant's thunder;" and in fact, has recreated the issue of the case.

Another example of developing a theme from negative facts occurs when representing a client who has many skeletons in his closet. A theme in this type of case may appear as follows:

> The defense counsel will put into evidence that my client has committed three different felonies. The defense counsel will do this in hopes of leading you away from a just result in this case. Yes, my client has had problems in the past, but those are behind him—he has paid his debt to society. In fact, my client pleaded guilty to those past crimes because, as he told the judge, he knew he had done the wrong thing and had to pay for his mistakes. Now he comes into this court on the right side. He was injured because the defendant was negligent. As a juror you are an officer of this Court, and it is your duty to decide this case based on the evidence and the law and nothing more. While the defense counsel has the right to present evidence on the criminal record of my client, it has absolutely nothing to do with who caused this accident or the extent of my client's injuries. When my client broke the law, he willingly accepted his punishment because he knew he was wrong. Wouldn't it be a strange system of justice if he could not depend on the law to be fair to him now, and compensate him when someone did something wrong to him?

### Presenting Your Theme Logically and Consistently

When preparing your case, think about the concept of reading a book about the life of an individual written by four separate authors. Each author has been told to write about a different stage in the individual's life. There is no general theme. The book would be as interesting and

18

effective as a trial conducted by four different attorneys, none of whom knew what the other was doing. It would have no central theme—and would not win over the jury.

Every part of your trial must contribute to a consistent theme. This might require that certain evidence that appears to be extremely strong and helpful to your client must be discarded because it is not consistent with that theme. For example, let's say, the defendant is a major corporation, and your theme is that this corporation is a moneymaking body that is indifferent about inflicting harm on the public. Your theme is to attack the board of directors for having agreed to put a given product out for sale to the general public. You may have evidence that one of the laborers for this corporation committed a horrible act that contributed to creating this horrible product. However, if the evidence of this laborer's act does not contribute to your theme of the board of directors causing the incident because of greed, and in fact lessens the impact, you should disregard it.

Consistency with the theme of your case is one of the most difficult concepts of trial practice to fully appreciate. Every part of your case, as stated, should logically fit into your theme. It is very difficult not to introduce all the favorable evidence, but this is crucial in presenting an effective theme. The theme presented must be logical and consistent, so there will be no confusion in the message you are attempting to convey. Moreover, as will be emphasized later in this book, it is very important to try to present as short and concise a case as possible. This often requires choosing what evidence to present and not to present.

## Chapter 3
## STYLISTIC ISSUES IN CLOSING

### Talking to Jurors as Friends

Great politicians give great speeches, but there are probably few of them who would make good trial lawyers. The technique used in persuading masses of people is different from that used in talking to and persuading a small group of people such as a jury. Many of America's most effective politicians are physically attractive, and they often have a speaking style and a voice that people find pleasant. The good news is that the trial lawyer's effectiveness is not dependent on physical attractiveness or a pleasant voice. Many of the most effective trial lawyers probably could not get elected to any political office but are nevertheless effective in persuading a jury. The difference between these two effective speakers is that one uses a formal, guarded approach to speech while the other is speaking candidly to jurors as friends, bringing them into the conversation, and making them a part of events taking place around them.

The closing argument must never be a speech. Rather, it should sound and feel as if someone were telling a friend about the incident, the issues, and the law. When speaking with a friend, a person does not talk down to him; otherwise they will not remain friends for very long. You should be relaxed and natural. A trial lawyer should not try to copy someone else's mannerisms and style. The same tone of voice, facial expressions, and body language used in explaining a position to a friend should be used in making the closing argument to the jury.

*Learning the Speech*

As stated previously, the closing argument should be prepared well in advance of the actual presentation, with modifications being incorporated throughout trial. You should practice the delivery of the closing argument several times, and probably should practice it in front of a non-lawyer and ask for comments. After all, you will be talking to non-lawyers when you deliver the closing argument, and a critique from a non-lawyer could be very helpful.

The best approach for most attorneys is a combination of "learning" the closing argument and using notes. If you are reading your closing arguments, you probably are losing more than your fair share of trials. There are many reasons for that; the least of which is that it is virtually impossible to ever "connect" with a jury that is simply watching you read your notes. It is impossible to ever develop any "peripheral vision" for what is occurring in the courtroom. You might as well type up your words, hand a copy to the jury, and ask them to "read it with feeling" as you sit and watch your case go down the tubes.

Professional actors are required to learn thousands of words as they perform their craft. The TelePrompTer in front of them is merely a mechanism that helps them remember key points. Even without that TelePrompTer, the most skillful actors playing key roles can deliver thousands of words without any written memory mechanisms at all. There are many memory tricks they use that you should consider. Sometimes they write and rewrite their lines with pen and paper. Sometimes they list key words for themselves that help them move from one paragraph of speech to another. Sometimes they create outlines that they can visualize as they deliver their lines. But the one thing they all recognize for sure is that they can never deliver a line creatively, insightfully, with feeling, until it is first learned, and they practice delivering it with different feelings and emotions.

Once a closing is learned, a lawyer can then be spontaneous and deliver big picture concepts in an impromptu way that looks natural and unrehearsed. Only after the key lines are learned through hard work can the lawyer really move around the concepts and master the concepts in a way that makes his work look like art. After learning the material, the key words or thoughts may be placed on note cards for use at trial. If the preparation is adequate, it is unlikely that a trial lawyer will need to continuously refer to notes. Instead, he will find himself "talking" to the jury. More important, the trial lawyer will know the material well enough to make adjustments according to what occurs during trial.

### Strongest Points First or Last

You should present your strongest points either first or last, but not in the middle. This is because people naturally remember more of what they hear first and last. However, if plaintiff's counsel believes that the opposing counsel cannot present any proof on a particular strong point, plaintiff's counsel should save this point for the end of the initial closing, and issue a strong, definite challenge to opposing counsel to address these issues sometime in his argument. The challenge should be written up on a board for the jury to remember and focus on as the opposing counsel delivers his argument.

For example, the authors handled a case involving a scuba diver who experienced a severe case of the bends and was taken to a hospital emergency room. At the time the diver entered the emergency room, he was not paralyzed, and there was an available Navy hyperbaric chamber located within ten minutes of the hospital. For reasons alleged by the defendants, the hospital flew the diver forty-five minutes to another hospital for treatment rather than take the diver to the Navy chamber. The diver ended up permanently paralyzed. The authors argued that the delay in treatment caused the paralysis, and the hospital argued that the diver had such a severe case of the bends that he was going to end up paralyzed no matter what. Moreover, the hospital claimed that the diver needed specialty care not available at the Navy chamber.

It is true that the diver had experienced an extremely severe case of the bends. However, the defense additionally chose to argue in opening statement and throughout trial that the diver would have ended up paralyzed even if he had been sent to the Navy chamber. The evidence did not support this defense statement. In fact, not one doctor or diving expert had ever seen a person go into a hyperbaric chamber not paralyzed and then come out paralyzed. For this reason, at the end of the opening portion of plaintiff's closing, the authors said the following:

I am about to sit down, and the attorneys for Pensacola Hospital are about to get up and make their closing argument. I have one question for Pensacola Hospital, and it is the one question that is crucial to the outcome of this case and your verdict. It is the question that the attorneys for Pensacola Hospital need to get up right now and immediately answer for you. The question is that not one single doctor or diving expert has ever seen a person go into a hyperbaric chamber not paralyzed and then come out paralyzed. It is clear that Keith Smith was not paralyzed when he was in the Pensacola Hospital emergency room, and it is also clear that there was an available hyperbaric chamber ten minutes away, and the medical personnel at this chamber were ready to accept and treat Keith. The question for Pensacola Hospital is: Isn't it true that if Pensacola Hospital had sent Keith Smith to the Navy chamber, Keith would not be paralyzed today? This is the question that the lawyers for Pensacola Hospital need to answer right now.

The attorneys for Pensacola Hospital did not answer this question or attempt to answer this question. The problem was that there was no answer to the question in light of the way the evidence came in at trial. The defense had created an issue before trial and during opening statement that proved unsupportable, and so we decided to make this one of the crucial issues in the case in closing argument. It is likely that many of the jurors were constantly thinking the whole time during the defense closing, "When is he going to answer this question?" When defense counsel was unable to answer the question, it certainly had to stick with the jurors during deliberations. Of course, in the rebuttal argument, the authors emphasized that the defense could not provide an answer, as it is clear that Mr. Smith would not be paralyzed today had he simply been sent to the Navy chamber.

The jury returned a $32 million verdict.

### *Style of Speaking*

It is critical for counsel to convey a belief that his position is unshakeable. He must be confident and sincere, and he must convey the seriousness of the case. He must avoid demonstrating a lack of confidence in his case, issues, or client. As stated by Alexander Hamilton, "the law is that which has been confidently asserted and boldly maintained." You may borrow another attorney's arguments, but you should never attempt to borrow his style. You should be yourself. You should use repetition and pauses to emphasize important points.

Finally, counsel must believe in what he is saying, and feel confident in what is said, without being flippant or cocky. Being well prepared is the best way for a lawyer to feel confident during trial and during closing argument. Becoming fully prepared for trial requires a significant shift in the attorney's attitude over the course of the preparatory period. During initial preparation, the attorney must adopt an overly critical and objective attitude in order to prepare every facet of the case. The attorney who is blindly confident rather than obsessively objective throughout preparation will tend to belittle the opposition's strong points and fail to appreciate the weaknesses of his own case. Force yourself to nitpick. Force yourself to obsess about details. Force yourself to be the worst critic of your case during the initial case preparation.

After completing the initial preparation, however, the time for objectivity ceases. The practitioner then must develop a frame of mind that is totally committed to the client's position. The attorney must believe in that position in order to convey it in its best light to the jury. It stands to reason that a person who actually believes in a cause can present it better than one who has doubts or a nagging worry that perhaps even he might believe in the opponent's case. This shift from objectivity to advocacy is a difficult shift that must be understood by a trial lawyer. We must be as capable in the role of objective critical analyst as we are in the role of unfaltering advocate.

### Speaking with Mental Images

The trial attorney should also create mental pictures to describe the facts. For example, besides stating that the plaintiff is a quadriplegic, counsel should also state that plaintiff cannot use his arms or legs. It is imperative that you leave mental pictures about what your words actually represent. The mental pictures are what the jurors will remember long after they hear your words.

One of the many legends about a very well-known trial lawyer from New York named Moe Levine is that he delivered these words during the rebuttal portion of his closing argument:

> You have heard a very capable lawyer tell you how the amputation of my client's arms is something that he will overcome with proper rehabilitation. Let me tell you what I have observed about my client. I had lunch with him today before we came into this courtroom for these arguments. He sat there

without his arms, bent his upper body down toward his plate and ate the food off his plate like a dog.

Although we are rarely given facts that allow us to leave mental pictures as powerful as this, we must constantly be vigilant in reducing our words to mental pictures that outlast our spoken words. Once you incorporate this concept into your speaking style, the use of such images will become more natural and more second nature.

### Use of Analogies in Closing Argument

Analogies are a very powerful form of argument and can be very effective in persuading a jury. Few persuasive devices affect jurors more than an appropriate comparison to something they recognize as true from their own personal knowledge and experience. Empirical research has shown that analogies assist jurors in recalling arguments better since they are remembered more than recitations of fact or logic. Analogies also help jurors to accept notions they might otherwise resist, and tend to exert a decisive role in influencing the conduct and direction of discussion during jury deliberations.

In one of the authors' cases, the defendant doctor created a false medical record a year after the incident. That medical record perfectly and uniquely supported the defendant's theory of the case. The argument was made in closing that the most compelling evidence of liability was the dishonest creation of the fraudulent medical record.

The fraudulent record became a metaphor for cheating, lying, and dishonesty that begins to sound very similar to criminal conduct. It is similar to the individual who runs from the scene of the crime as the police arrive. The flight alone is an admission of guilt just as powerful as the defendant stating he committed the crime. Why would the defendant run from the scene unless he had done something wrong? Why did the defendant create a medical record one year after the incident, unless he knew he had done something wrong and needed evidence to support his position?

## Use of Rhetorical Questions in Closing Arguments

Rhetorical questions can be a very effective tool if used properly, and if the answer to the rhetorical question is absolutely clear. You need to remember that a rhetorical question is a question that clearly answers itself. Thus, make sure the question only has one answer, and that it is immediately clear to every juror.

The authors often end the opening portion of their closing argument by issuing a rhetorical question to the defense counsel. For example, counsel may state: "I am about to sit down, and [Mr. Defense Counsel] will have the opportunity to deliver his closing argument. [Mr. Defense Counsel] needs to immediately answer the question: 'If [defense doctor] did not believe he committed malpractice on Mr. Smith, then why would he create a fraudulent medical record one year after the incident?'" This type of rhetorical question is very effective at placing the opposing counsel on the defensive as he begins his closing. The rhetorical question should be such, however, that it cannot be explained, and the rhetorical question should be central to your theme. As the opposing counsel begins his closing argument, the jury is expecting an immediate answer to the rhetorical question. Yet the authors have never witnessed one incident where opposing counsel did in fact even address the question.

If you are ever faced with this type of rhetorical question, and your opponent has done an excellent job, and there is no effective way to respond to the rhetorical question, you may want to argue the following:

As you realize, we lawyers are limited in the time that we have. My opponent has gone through and selected a number of questions that would require me to spend all of my time answering. There are only two questions that need to be answered in this case, and he should have answered those instead of trying to get me to spend my limited time answering some questions that he has concocted. The two questions that should be answered and that he should have answered are those that are contained in the jury instructions and verdict form. He doesn't want to answer those questions. So I say to my opponent that I am not going to spend my time answering his questions. I'm going to spend my time answering the questions that the Court will ask because it is the questions that the Court will ask you to answer in the jury instructions and verdict form that are the important questions. What are these questions? . . .

## Use of Visual Aids in Closing Arguments

Cognitive science has shown that most of what is forgotten is forgotten immediately after it is first learned; then the rate of forgetting slows. A number of variables have been identified that contribute to the rate of forgetting and retention: for example, the learning environment itself; how well the new material correlates with what has previously been learned about the subject; recentness of exposure to the new information; opportunity for mental rehearsal; and availability of retrieval cues. Understanding, retention, and retrieval of material can be increased significantly by combining the visual and verbal channels.

Retention and comprehension are increased when jurors are shown and told something instead of just hearing words that probably become confused in their memory. This is especially true in today's time where people are overwhelmed with visual information from television, movies, the internet, and high-tech computer presentations. Therefore, attorneys should integrate audio-visual aids with their key issues. Common visual aids include enlarged portions of the trial transcript testimony, enlarged photographs, medical illustrations, timelines, computer animations, computer presentations such as PowerPoint slides, digital video segments, and the use of a visual presenter machine. The authors have used each of these types of visual aids during closing and have found them very effective.

Visual aids, however, should be used only for the most important issues that must be retained by the jury. Overuse of visual aids will confuse the jury as to what is important, and some of the most important issues may be overlooked. It is also important to keep the visual aids concise and simple. It is not uncommon for high-tech presentations to fail because the visual aids are so impressive-looking and professional that the jurors lose sight of the actual message being conveyed. High-tech presentations also can give the appearance that the opposing counsel's case must be weak on the facts if he feels it necessary to spend so much money creating "a dog and pony show" or a "smoke and mirror show" that appears to be far "too slick" for the setting.

It is also important to carefully review all visual aids before providing them to opposing counsel. This is especially true of computer animations. We have been involved in trials where we were able to utilize opposing counsel's visual aids to prove vital points in our case. If the visual aid is not such that it truly helps your case in explaining the issues to the jury, then do not use the aid. The substance of your presentation is more important than the form.

### Use of Video Deposition Cuts and Trial Transcript Cuts

Once a jury retires to the jury room to deliberate, probably the one item the jurors ask for more than any other is a trial transcript. If you have read deposition transcripts into the record, the jurors generally believe they should be entitled to those transcribed words back in the jury room. Most courts do not allow transcripts to be sent back to the jury room. Thus, it is important for you to highlight the key testimony during closing argument.

The authors use a combination of ways to convey trial testimony during closing. One is to simply blow-up portions of the trial transcript and paste them on cardboard backings and display them before the jury and read them. A second way is to type the relevant questions and answers into a PowerPoint presentation that you utilize during closing. A third way is to actually have clips from video depositions played during closing. This is especially helpful when the deponent's facial expressions and body language speak volumes more than the spoken word.

The most important thing is to make sure that you use portions of the transcripts during closing and that you do it in such a way that the jury can actually see or witness the actual spoken words. Do not merely tell the jury that Mr. Jones said this and Ms. Smith said that.

### Should the Argument Be Logical or Emotional?

The answer to this question depends on how the trial has proceeded, and how the lawyers and parties have come across. Generally, from a plaintiff's lawyer's standpoint, the opening portion of closing argument should be very logical and unemotional. It is the rebuttal portion of closing argument where the plaintiff should begin to show signs of righteous indignation and turn up the level of emotion. The artful use of emotion in closing can have a powerful impact on the way a jury processes facts. However, you also need to consider the fact that in your career as a lawyer, you will hear more than a few stories where the emotional appeal by a plaintiff's lawyer actually brought tears to the eyes of the jury, and yet the jury still delivered a zero verdict for the plaintiff.

It is important for you to determine whether or not an emotional argument fits your demeanor. Nothing is more ineffective and ridiculous-looking than a lawyer who attempts to make use of an emotional argument when his true, more comfortable demeanor is driven more by an organized, calculated, logical argument. In other words, if it doesn't fit, then don't force it. Pounding on a podium with a raised voice is not the type of delivery that works for everyone. The way the message is delivered must look like it actually belongs to the messenger. The way you choose to change your pace of speaking and your tone of speaking must be natural, as it is often just as important as the words you choose to speak.

The most difficult summation for a plaintiff's lawyer is when the defense counsel and the defendant have come across as logical, matter-of-fact, pleasant, and straightforward people. From a defense attorney perspective, the attorney should generally keep the argument logical and not rely on an overly emotional presentation. The defense attorney should avoid giving the plaintiff's counsel the opportunity to capitalize on an emotional argument in rebuttal. Moreover, an argument based on logical, matter-of-fact, and unemotional appeals often causes the jurors themselves to become less emotional, and more juror-like, and less likely to return an excessive verdict.

### Humor in Closing Argument

Recent studies show that while a minority of jurors do not mind a few jokes in the courtroom, most jurors prefer a no-nonsense approach. This is especially true in closing argument. Jokes are almost never appropriate during closing, and, as a general rule, humor is rarely appropriate, as this is not a time when the plaintiff's counsel should give the jury the impression that the setting is unimportant, trivial, and casual.

The trial is now at an end, and the jury must begin deliberations. It is a serious and important time. This is not to suggest that the lawyer should be overly grave and formal. The lawyer always needs to be balanced, sensitive, caring, and easy for the jury to relate to. It is helpful for the jurors to actually like the lawyer, but this impression must be formed before the closing. If something occurred in trial that is humorous and you have the opportunity to mention it without patronizing the jury or trivializing the setting, then it may be appropriate to mention it to show the jury that you have a sense of humor even when faced with a very serious and important situation. If the jury smiles, then this might be an indication that the jurors are receptive to you and your case. If the jurors do not smile, this is typically an indication they are not receptive to you, and you will certainly want to state that the case is not about the personalities of the lawyers, but about the facts and the law.

You will find very few trial lawyers during your career who have a knack for using humor during any part of a trial, much less the closing argument. As a rule, if it does not feel natural for you, then don't try.

### Should You Ever Compliment Opposing Counsel?

There is certainly nothing wrong with deserved compliments. One of the worst things that a lawyer can do at trial, however, is to give the jury the impression that he is insincere or not truthful. To compliment opposing counsel when it is not deserved is a mistake. One of the worst decisions one of the authors ever received was many years ago when he complimented an older attorney who was obviously way beyond his days of competency. Afterwards, one of the jurors commented that he thought the author was not only disrespectful but was making fun of the older gentleman because the compliment seemed forced, insincere, and inappropriate, and the juror immediately recognized that.

What do you do when it appears one or more jurors are intrigued by or enamored by opposing counsel? For example, opposing counsel may have very limited talent but be attractive and charming. The best way to approach this problem is to face it head-on, which is the answer to every problem contained in this book. The following is a sample response to this situation:

> The lawyers in this case are not on trial. My opponent is one of the most likeable people that any one of us would want to meet. You have seen him in court, and he is charming. But that is not what this case is about. You took an oath that you would judge this case on the evidence and the law. You can imagine how wrong it would be if there was a crotchety old lawyer on one side of the case who did not have a lot of personality, but had the law and evidence on his side, but on the other side was a very personable lawyer who had no case. It would not be justice if the jury made decisions based on whether they liked the lawyer or not. That would be more like a beauty contest than a jury trial in a court of law. You all took an oath that you would judge the case solely on the facts and the law. Our system of justice is based on the principle that we must judge our peers blindfolded. We cannot see race, religion, gender, wealth, nationality, or personality. We must see only the facts and the law.

### Should You Ever Call A Witness or a Party a Liar or a Fraud?

The answer depends on the circumstances. If you are going to call someone a liar, make certain that it is obvious that the witness or party did lie. If there is a chance that someone might easily construe that the witness was confused, you stand the chance of unnecessarily offending the jury. You also run the risk that your opponent will take advantage of it in his argument. Of course, even if a party or witness lied, you never attack him if the witness is likeable.

If you perceive that the jury did not like the witness and it was obvious that the witness lied or changed records, you have the right (in most jurisdictions) to call the witness a liar and to attempt to characterize the opposing side's entire case as a lie. We suggest something as follows:

We are all striving for justice. The jury system is the greatest legal system ever devised. In order to be assured that justice occurs, however, everyone must tell the truth when he is under oath. No one should destroy evidence or change evidence or lie. When this occurs, it is up to the jury to determine the truth. That is your job when you retire to the juryroom.

To tell the truth or to present truthful evidence by not destroying evidence or changing evidence is such a simple concept. You do not need the law to tell you that a witness who is under oath should not lie or that someone should not change a record. This not only violates our law; it violates our morality. It violates what our entire society is based upon. It is one of those rules that most of us learned as children. It is one of those rules about living that is as old as the Bible itself.

Why would a person lie or change a record? There is only one reason. He knows he did wrong, and he is trying to prevent the truth from being discovered. Lying and destruction of evidence are the same as an admission of guilt. It is the same as running from the scene of a crime. There is no reason to run from the scene of a crime unless you are guilty.

If it is not appropriate to call the witness a liar without risking offending the jury, you must find a more polite manner in which to address this issue. There was an outstanding trial lawyer by the name of Louis Nizer, who practiced law in New York City for almost seventy years. He attributed all of his trial skills to something called the "Rule of Probability." He stated that jurors, based on their common experiences, will anticipate how people should react under a given set of circumstances. This is also referred to as a person's logical reaction and response to an event. The authors are believers in the "Rule of Probability" and have often stated:

> We know that the mere fact that somebody says something or testifies to something that is illogical or improbable doesn't mean the person necessarily is lying. The issue is whether the witness is testifying to an improbable act or an improbable explanation. For example, if a person comes up to a stop sign that he has stopped at 1,000 times, but does not stop this time; then this would be an improbable act. It does not make sense, but we can accept that it occurred.

> But let's say that the driver of the vehicle who ran the stop sign leaves the scene of the collision and runs into his home or a bar and begins drinking alcohol. If the driver testifies that he left the scene in order to get the injured party help and began drinking alcohol to calm his nerves, this is not logical; and it is most likely untrue. Logic would tell you that there was a good chance that the driver had been drinking before the collision, and his drinking is what caused him to run the stop sign.

> Let's look at all the illogical statements made in this case. . . .

> It is against common sense that all of these illogical events could have occurred. It is possible that one illogical event can take place, and maybe two, but not all of these events.

> Well, what does this mean? It means that if these things are not true, then the defendant knew they were not true. Why would he say something under oath that is stretching the truth? Common sense tells us that someone would not stretch the truth unless he believed that the person he was telling this to would

believe the story. In this case, the fact that he acted negligently and caused injury to another person is bad enough. The fact that he would try to convince a jury of his position by stretching the truth is an insult to our system of justice.

It was bad conduct that caused the injury to the plaintiff, but it was calculated and intentional misconduct that made matters much worse by telling this illogical, improbable story of how it occurred.

### *Understanding the Boundaries of What You Can and Cannot Say*

In the last five years, many appellate courts have been quick to interfere with jury decisions when lawyers have made arguments that include words, thoughts, and/or suggestions that the appellate courts have proclaimed to be inappropriate.

The truth is that many of these appellate decisions border on what can only be characterized as absurdly naïve; but they nevertheless exist, and we must be aware of them when delivering our closing arguments.

Some of the ideas and arguments suggested in this book may border on unethical and/or reversible error depending upon the law in your specific jurisdiction. What may be proper argument in Cook County, Illinois, may not be proper in Tallahassee, Florida.

For this reason, the authors have included a chapter in this book that reviews judicial activism at its best and worst depending on your personal beliefs. Make sure you develop your arguments in compliance with the laws of your jurisdiction.

## Chapter 4
## FACTS AND ISSUES THAT ARE A PROBLEM
## FOR YOUR CASE

By the end of trial, you should be able to recognize the various problems that could lead a jury to find against your client. For example, your client may have come across poorly, a juror may have developed a dislike for you or may be intrigued by opposing counsel, or the jury may not be able to relate to your client or sympathize with your client. The best way to handle these potential problems is to address them head-on and present those points in a much better light than you will hear coming from the mouth of your opponent.

### Being the First to Spin

In the outback of Australia, the ostrich has one of the highest mortality rates of most all the other odd-looking creatures running around in those parts. The reason is that the ostrich is inordinately slow to react to predators that have an intention of making the huge feathered creature into their next meal. Ostriches have the ability to react and to save themselves, but more often than not, they become prey.

That same scenario too often plays itself out in courtrooms where one trial lawyer has become prey to another, and the prey is unwilling to react in time to save himself or his client. Trial lawyers must learn to quickly and effectively respond to all serious, and even minimal, problems that arise before and during trial. The lawyer who learns to put the best spin on a problem will ultimately succeed.

The following two arguments illustrate this concept.

The first case involved a wealthy lawyer's wife who was injured in an automobile accident. The defense attorney did his best to prejudice the jury against the client by constantly emphasizing the client's financial condition and the occupation of her husband. As the trial progressed, it was apparent that the defense's attack was working. Here's how the problem was handled:

What is this case about? It is very simple. It is about a person who, through no fault of her own, sustained a very serious injury to her leg. She has undergone seven surgeries. She has attended physical therapy on 120 occasions. She has had x-rays performed on her leg on twenty-seven different occasions, and she has been to a doctor more than sixty times. Also, every single doctor agrees that her leg is not healed, and she needs another surgery.

What is this case not about? This case is not about the fact that Mr. Smith is an attorney or that he makes a comfortable living or that he and his wife own a Mercedes and a Volvo and a Suburban. It is not about the fact that the Smiths have a two-bedroom cabin in Alabama, or they have a boat, or that Mrs. Smith has not had to work in twenty years. I spoke with you about this in jury selection, and everyone agreed that the justice system must be blind. It must be blind to race, religion, gender, nationality, and wealth. It should not matter whether someone is black or white, whether a person is female or male, whether a person is American or not, or whether a person has income or not.

It is very difficult for many to sympathize with Mrs. Smith. She has been married twenty-two years. Her husband has a good job.

She has three healthy children. She has a home she has lived in for more than twenty years, and her husband makes a good income. In fact, the defense read one hour of deposition testimony from its surveillance people from Atlanta to testify that they followed Mrs. Smith around and saw her in a Mercedes, Volvo, and Suburban. They didn't say they saw her playing tennis, or jogging, or playing sports, or boating, or doing gardening. They put on a video surveillance tape to show Mrs. Smith driving a Mercedes, and then put on a surveillance tape showing her driving a Volvo, and then finally put on a surveillance tape showing her driving a Suburban.

Why do you think the defense put on these videos? It certainly wasn't for the purpose of showing you that Mrs. Smith had great use of her leg. They wanted you to know that the Smiths owned three vehicles.

When you think about this, the defense is trying to directly appeal to any potential prejudices that a juror may have against people who have money. That is not right. That is not our judicial system, and not the American system of justice.

Here is another example of a case where it was critically important to spin first:

In this case, Wayne Jones was the exact opposite of Mrs. Smith. Mr. Jones had never earned more than $10,000 per year, and that occurred only when he was able to hold full-time employment. He and his family were often homeless, without food or clothes, and sometimes lived out of an automobile. Mr. Jones was killed as a result of Wal-Mart's negligence. The following is a portion of the damage argument in which we take these negative facts and try to turn them into a positive. The trial resulted in a multimillion-dollar jury verdict:

I would like you to consider the following when thinking about damages. Wayne Jones met Sandra Jones and married her one month later. Over the next eleven years, he had to deal with her severe mental illness, deal with his son's hyperactivity, and deal with losing his job on the police force. He was homeless and without food and clothes. He was living out of cars with his family. Yet he never walked away or gave up on his family. How easy it would have been for him to wake up one day and say, "It's over, bye, I'm gone," and to move away, and find himself a job making minimum wage, and meet someone else, and to have walked out on his responsibilities and his family.

But Wayne Jones never did this. Wayne never gave up hope that life would get better. Wayne did not turn to drugs, and he did not turn to crime. Wayne had a tremendous gift. He understood the loyalty of family and understood the importance of not giving up even when life is very cruel and tough. He continued to try to assist his family and give them a better life, despite his enormous weaknesses. Sandra, Christopher, and Michelle will never find such a loyal and understanding individual as Wayne Jones, a person who stood by them no matter what, and a person who would have taught them how to face adversity head-on and without fear.

Jurors take their job very seriously, and they want to do the right thing. Therefore, it is best to address all problems head-on and remind the jurors about the difficulty and seriousness of their job. Their job is not to be swayed by prejudices and preconceived notions and beliefs. It is not to be swayed by the physical attractiveness of the attorneys or clients. It is not to be swayed by sympathy for one side or the other. Their job is simply to judge the facts and to apply the law.

Do not hide the hand you have been dealt. By addressing all problem issues head-on, and reminding the jurors of their sworn responsibility, you will compel the jury to focus on the facts and the law and reach a decision guided by these issues alone.

## Overcoming the Appeal to Cynicism

Many defense attorneys are masters at bringing out the worst in a jury. They are able to pander to all of the very worst character traits that often surface within the lives of individuals who make up a jury. It is often their goal to focus on all of mankind's very worst characteristics, such as greed, loathsomeness, and dishonesty, and visit those qualities upon your client.

It is easy for the defense to accomplish this because we are trying cases during a time when jurors want to believe the worst about you, your case, and your client. Detractors of the American civil justice system have been hugely successful in creating an image of claimants and claimants' lawyers that is tough to overcome. It is even more difficult to overcome when your opponent is able to create a mind-set for the jury that you and your client are simply a living example of everything they have heard that is bad about our civil justice system. The defense leads the jurors to believe that you and your client are in the courtroom for all the greedy reasons they have heard about long before they were ever chosen to be jurors. Their worst cynicism surfaces and the courtroom becomes the symbol of a temple of greed.

Here is an example of the type of argument that you should consider in dealing with the problem preemptively in your closing:

Ladies and gentlemen: As I have watched this trial unfold this week, I have seen something that is disturbing. I have seen counsel for the defendant, in a series of small ways, try to cause cynicism to rise up in each of us as individuals. Not the type of cynicism that leads us to honestly and impartially evaluate the facts and evidence, but the type of cynicism that takes our

41

humanity, our compassion, our impartiality, and our wisdom away from us and leaves us feeling hatred and resentment. You see, defense counsel began pandering to cynicism in voir dire when he made an issue out of the fact that my law firm advertises. He was hoping that you would conclude that I was somehow unworthy to be appearing in front of you in this trial. He was hoping that you would see me as an ambulance-chasing low-life trying to earn money by drumming up frivolous lawsuits. What do I say about this? I say that if you find that this lawsuit is frivolous, then you do the right thing and find against my client. However, if you find that this case is legitimate and my client has the right to seek remedy for the harm caused to her, then also do the right thing and don't hold my firm's advertisements against my client. This case is not about my firm. It is about my client.

Let me tell you how else counsel for the defense was hoping that he could cause your cynicism to overcome your ability to follow the law and your ability to sit as a fair juror in this case. He did it with the series of questions that he asked my client and the witnesses. They were questions that, at every turn, made it somehow look like my client was only here out of greed. That somehow, my client was not doing all he could do to improve his life. That somehow, my client saw this process as some sick, distorted game of Lotto. That somehow, it is my client's fault that he lost the use of his right leg. You see, counsel for the defense created those images because he wanted you to ignore the law, ignore the facts of this case, and bring out every sense of negativity that he believes may be stored up in your heart.

There is no room for undue distrust in the process of a jury trial. Not everything is perfect about the American justice system, but it is a civil justice system that is the envy of the world. It is not a system that has lasted 200 years because it has been driven by undue cynicism. It is today the envy of the world because it is a system that abandons our prejudices, our biases, our cynical views of the world, and allows us to judge each case based on the facts and the evidence presented, and the law.

### Addressing the Negative Image of Lawyers and Frivolous Lawsuits

Throughout the last decade, plaintiffs' lawyers have, more often than not, been too willing to cave in on the defense lawyer attacks that center around frivolous lawsuits and the damage they cause to the civil justice system.

It is a defense that cannot be ignored because unfortunately this is an idea that the public is quick to accept. There has always been, and always will be, a legion of marginally talented lawyers who believe it enhances their personal career to file and pursue overreaching lawsuits.

Like it or not, there is a plausibility, a believability to the defense argument that frivolous and absurd lawsuits are undermining our civil justice system. The hard truth is that the vast majority of potential jurors believe that the system does not work because of frivolous lawsuits.

However, that does not mean that we should always be quick to allow the defense attorney's attacks to go unanswered. In fact, you should always be conscious of the fact that, in the right setting, with the right facts and the right defense counsel, you can turn this defense into an affirmative attack that you use in your closing. If the defense counsel and the defendant he represents do not have the talent, appeal, or character to hold onto the high ground with such an argument, you should take the opportunity to consider the following for your rebuttal closing:

During the very beginning of this trial, the defendant's lawyer brought up how some lawyers and some juries are harming the civil justice system with their silly lawsuits. He talked to you about the McDonald's hot coffee case and the verdict the jury reached in that case. But what he didn't talk about are the facts of that case. He didn't talk about the hundreds of people severely burned by McDonald's coffee because McDonald's wanted to save money on free refills because the coffee could not be consumed as quickly. He didn't talk about the fact that the lady's doctor testified that she had suffered the worst burns that he had ever seen. And he didn't talk about the fact that McDonald's corrected the problem, and people stopped being needlessly burned all because a jury told McDonald's it was wrong.

The defendant's lawyer talked about the McDonald's case because he wanted you to blindly focus on the negative aspects of the jury system. I will be one of the first to admit that the jury system is not perfect. Mistakes are made, but the jury system in America is the best system possible. Juries throughout history have bravely faced the most powerful people, companies, and governmental entities throughout the world and held them accountable. Juries have brought about changes in the workplace. They have brought about changes that have improved medication, automobiles, toys, the environment, hospitals, and nursing homes. Juries have stood up when the national and state governments chose to sit down.

Jury decisions have had a far greater impact on safety than the actions of all the national and state regulators, all the politicians, and all the bureaucrats put together. And unlike what this company's lawyer wants you to believe, there is nothing wrong, silly, or frivolous about what lawyers and civil juries do every day in this country. The thousands of people who have been hurt by bad products and the thousands of people whose lives have been saved by the actions of civil juries aren't laughing. They are thankful. They don't believe there is anything silly or frivolous about our justice system and its lawyers. When this trial is over today, you will get into your car that is safer than it was one hundred lawsuits ago, and on your way home you will drive through stop lights and cross train tracks that are safer than they were one hundred lawsuits ago. And hopefully, when you see the connection between positive change and the civil justice system, you will agree that there is nothing silly or frivolous about my client and the impact your decision may have.

### *Inconsistent Statements and Inconsistent Records: The Shortcoming of Being Human*

So many times we have seen cases lost because the client or a witness said something during trial, in a deposition, or to a doctor that was inconsistent with the evidence and the truth. Again, you should not try to make these inconsistent statements consistent with some ridiculous explanation. Do not make the problem worse by arguing something that is implausible. Simply tell the truth, and discuss what each and every person knows. That is, everyone makes mistakes. This is especially true when the inconsistency is in a deposition where many people find themselves deathly afraid of the legal system and what they perceive as lawyer trickery. Each of us has seen an eyewitness who was questioned about how long it took for some event to take place and the witness says "a couple of minutes," when in fact it was a few seconds. Each of us can recall witnesses making estimates of one hundred yards when it was really fifty or sixty feet. How do you handle this in argument? The same as every other problem; tell the truth and face the problem head on. You might try something as follows:

There is a saying among some lawyers that when the evidence is not in your favor, then rely upon the law. When the law is not in your favor, then rely upon the evidence. When neither the law nor the evidence is in your favor, then rely on lawyer talk. This is exactly what the defense is doing in this case, relying on lawyer talk. Lawyers are sometimes the masters of creating confusion where none really exists. The truth is, lawyers know that everyone is human, and therefore, mistakes are always going to be made. This has to be the case because people are not perfect. Therefore, if you get enough documents or talk to enough people, you are always going to get a little different version of how the accident happened, or what the injuries are, or how it affects the injured person. This has to be the case because we always say things a little differently every time we tell someone something. We always repeat something or write it down a little differently than it was told to us. People forget things or just don't think about things when being asked about it. In fact, people sometimes forget the names of family members or close friends.

And then by the time a trial like this takes place, we have every single record about everything that has ever occurred in a person's life. We have depositions of everyone who knows any detail about our case. Sometimes, those depositions are taken where people are pinned down about every possible detail they might remember. And as you might expect, they are a little fearful, they are a little confused, they are a little human, so they forget; they don't say things exactly right. They might be even too quick to speak as you have seen even the lawyers do during this trial. And, ladies and gentlemen; as lawyers, we have a responsibility not to stand before you and manipulate minor inconsistencies that aren't really important to the truth of this case. We have a responsibility to recognize that everyone in this courtroom is human. We all are subject to making mistakes. We owe each other as humans the decency and thoughtfulness of not treating each other as cheats and liars every time we get a detail wrong.

### Some Members of The Jury May Be Mad at You Personally: The Art of Falling on Your Sword

No matter how smooth, charismatic, or insightful you are as a trial lawyer, you are sometimes going to make jurors on your panel angry at you personally. Most of the time this will occur during your cross-examination of a witness they like. It will usually be a witness they feel some kinship with or a witness for whom they feel sympathy. You are also likely to anger jurors if they perceive that you have gotten too sideways with a judge that they might like, or even an opposing counsel that they favor. The easy, naïve thing to do is to act like the problem does not exist and merely hope for the best. It is risky to hope that those jurors will overcome their anger and merely decide your case according to the facts and the law. Most of the time that will be a disastrous gamble.

There is a principle in selling that also has a very direct application to trying a case. That principle is that you should speak out loud all of the negative thoughts your hearers have on their minds. In other words, if it is likely that your jury has a bias, then bring that bias to the surface by directly, affirmatively, honestly talking about that bias in your closing. The wisdom behind that approach is that a hidden bias, prejudice, resentment, or anger will begin to dissipate only when you begin to openly discuss the problem. Simply put, let them know that you know. Frank honesty is the beginning of any cathartic process. Jurors have a great capacity to forgive if you will help them. Here is an example of how to deal with the problem:

> Ladies and gentlemen, I know that some of you may be angry with me about the way I handled Dr. Jones on cross-examination. When I was asking him some of the questions I felt

as if I needed to ask, I think I might have even seen the anger on the faces of a few of you. This is my time to tell you that I am sorry if I made you angry. It is my time to tell you that for three years I have been doing my very best to help my client put her life back together by being the most capable advocate I could be, and I feel like I have let her down if I have made you angry during this trial. I was hard on Dr. Jones because I believed it was my obligation to my client to ask those tough questions, because my client could not stand up and ask those questions. She was relying on me to do that for her. So if I did wrong in your eyes in the way I did that, I hope you can forgive me; but more importantly, I ask you not to allow your anger with me to interfere with your fairness toward my client whose only day for compensation is today. She will never have another opportunity.

### *Jurors Deliberating on Facts and Evidence Not in the Record*

Jurors today are exposed to a tremendous amount of information about the legal process. Growing up, they have seen numerous television programs and movies involving lawyers. They hear details of high-profile cases on the news virtually every day. Jurors want to be Matlock-like investigators and uncover that smoking gun piece of evidence that nobody else sees in your case. They come to trial with their personal knowledge and life experiences, which they are dying to utilize in our case. This often results in the jurors discussing issues during deliberation that have never been addressed or ever thought about during trial. It is for this reason that we always state something similar to the following:

When you go back to reach your verdict, I would like you to remember something. That is, the lawyers on both sides of this case have been with this case for over three years. We know more about this case than the experts, the parties, or anyone else.

There is not a single piece of evidence that has not been researched and looked at by a number of people. You can be assured that if there were anything in any of the evidence that was of benefit to either side, it would have been pointed out. The reason I am saying this is that sometimes jurors will go back and one juror will point out something he read or something he saw and that was never pointed out by the attorneys, and sometimes the other jurors rely on this. When this happens, justice is not done because none of the attorneys are given a chance to respond, and it is very likely that there is a lot of other evidence or facts that would refute the juror's argument. The attorneys, however, chose not to put on this evidence because they knew the other side could easily refute it with additional evidence.

I would like you all to make a promise to me, and that is if anyone tries to go back to the jury room and rely upon anything other than the law or the facts presented in this trial, you stop them and tell them that it is not part of what you can consider. His Honor has instructed you only to consider the law and the facts presented in this trial.

### *Addressing the Issue of the Law Conflicting with a Juror's Personal Beliefs*

In virtually every case, there will be an issue that one or more jurors do not believe in for personal reasons and do not feel comfortable supporting. It is crucial that you explain to the jurors their responsibility to follow the law, even when the law conflicts with their beliefs. For this reason, we almost always state something as follows:

Before I sit down, I would like to talk about jury responsibility. As you can tell, we are asking for a lot of compensation from the defendant as a result of this incident. The amount of money we are talking about is so high that I spent a lot of time when we were picking a jury in this case to talk about how significant this case was. I told everyone that past medicals were $1,000,000 and that future medicals are $6,500,000. I also mentioned that future wage loss would be around $750,000. And I asked everyone could they award figures like this and also award a separate and even larger amount of compensation for pain and suffering and loss of enjoyment of life. And everyone started talking and being honest with the court, and some said, "I am sorry, I just can't follow the law regarding this. Even if the evidence showed that the past and future medicals total $7,500,000 and wage loss totals $750,000, I can't award this sum of money, and I especially cannot award any significant amount for pain and suffering and loss of enjoyment of life." I thanked each of these people for their honesty and openness because I knew if they had not spoken up, then it was possible that someone would be sitting on this jury today who could not put their personal feelings aside and award a sum of money required by law. And I knew when these people spoke out that the court would remove them from the panel because our system of justice requires that jurors put the law above everything else. And the reason for this is that our system of justice is based on a system of laws and not men. We don't have a system whereby juries get to consider a person's race, religion, age, gender, or wealth. Everyone is supposed to be treated equally under the law.

Everyone has seen the image we use to represent the idea of justice. Our Lady of Justice holds a balance scale in one hand, and she is always blindfolded. The reason she is blindfolded is because the jury is supposed to be blind to their personal beliefs when deciding a case, and the case must be decided based on the law. One of the most difficult tasks a person can do is to put away personal beliefs. In this case, there are several things that cannot be considered when reaching your verdict. For example, you cannot consider whether you like the defendant or not, or whether you had a good experience or bad experience with the defendant. You cannot consider whether you approve of the type of work my client did. You cannot consider which lawyer or party you liked better. And you cannot consider your personal beliefs on caps on damages or jury awards.

Probably any juror who has ever had to face the responsibility you face in this trial would tell you that absolutely the most difficult part of his or her job was not to sort through the complicated facts or having to concentrate nonstop for hours everyday. The most difficult part was having to put aside all of his or her personal beliefs; all of his or her preconceived ways of viewing the world; and to simply, unquestioningly, following the law even when he or she did not want to.

A juror who sits on a jury has taken an oath and promised everyone involved that he or she will follow the law. If we have proven to you that the law is such that my client is entitled to a lot of money, then please don't go back and reduce my client's compensation simply because we are talking about big numbers. A juror should be proud when he or she leaves jury service. A juror should be able to go to friends and relatives and say, "I don't know about what other juries have done or whether other awards were just, but I know that under the facts of this case and under the law that Mr. Jones was entitled to a very large award. Even if I personally disagree with awarding large sums of money, I am very proud to state that I followed the law."

### The Key Witness Who Has Been Discredited

One of your key witnesses has been significantly discredited during the trial. As stated previously, you cannot ignore negative facts or negative events. You must address them, and make them part of your theme. The following is a sample argument:

> As I told you at the start of the case, my opponent Mr. Smith is an outstanding lawyer. He hammered the witness, Mr. Simpson. As you recall, Mr. Simpson contradicted himself and his previous deposition. Mr. Simpson also became very hostile and upset on the witness stand, which made the matter worse.
>
> The question is whether Mr. Simpson lied or whether he was confused? If you believe he lied, then you should disregard everything he had to say. However, if you believe that he was confused and that this outstanding lawyer was able to make him look like a fool because he was confused, then you should not hold that against my client. If Mr. Smith did a great job of cross-examination, then give him an "A." Let him have this cross-examination typed up and used as an example of shrewd lawyering.
>
> But there is a difference between confusion and perjury. I submit to you that the witness was confused, and the more he tried to straighten out the matter and the more Mr. Smith was able to make him look silly, the madder the witness got. I'd suggest to you that the reason he got so mad was that he knew what the truth was. He wanted you to see the truth, but it was obvious that he felt that what he was trying to tell you was being manipulated somehow. There is nothing more frustrating than to know you're telling the truth and to have someone put a different slant on what you are trying to say.
>
> How do we know that Mr. Simpson was simply confused? Let's look at the other evidence in this case, and let's look at common sense and logic.

### *Explaining the Importance of the Decision*

It is crucial to remind the jurors of the importance of their decision, and the fact that their decision will have a lifelong impact on the parties. The following is a sample statement we have conveyed to juries:

> You have the power here today to determine what Andrew Wiley will be awarded for this incident. There will not be another jury that will have that power. Your decision today is the final word as to what Andrew will ever get. A famous person once said: "I can't do everything to solve the problems of others, but I must do what I can." You, the jury, cannot cure Andrew. You do not have the ability to make everything the same as it was. But you do have the ability to do the best you can for Andrew. You have the ability to provide the means for Andrew to get proper medical care, and to live the most normal life he will ever be able to. You have a tremendous responsibility today.
>
> Andrew has forty-eight more years of life according to the mortality tables. Therefore, in the year 2,055, Andrew will likely still be alive. While most of the people sitting in this courtroom today, including Andrew's parents, will likely have passed on, the decision you make today will determine what Andrew's life will be like in the year 2055 and what his life will be like for every year leading up to 2055.
>
> For the next forty-eight years, Andrew will either be at home with his parents or in a facility. During the time he is in a facility, there is no way to know who will be working with him, what their motivations might be, what their background might be. He must take the good with the bad. He is simply at the mercy of a system that can add quality to his life, a system that can improve his life or cause even more suffering for Andrew. Andrew can only be as happy and safe as the people caring for him allow him to be. Your decision today will guide who will care for Andrew

through the year 2055. Today, you are caring for Andrew. Today, Andrew is at your mercy.

### *Preserving the Notion That Your Case Is Unique*

It is often the plan of defense lawyers to make your case sound like it is just a run-of-the-mill, garden-variety case. The defense goal becomes one of diminishing the importance and uniqueness of the facts the jury has listened to throughout the trial. Your goal is to characterize the conduct of the corporation and the suffering it has caused as extraordinary and uncommon. The goal of the defense, however, is to make the facts of your case seem like just another boring, everyday occurrence in an American courtroom. In order to convey the uniqueness of our cases, the authors state something similar to the following:

> As I listened to the defense counsel's argument, he almost tried to make it sound like there is nothing unique or uncommon about the extraordinary facts of this case, and the unusual evidence you have heard and viewed in this trial throughout this week. I am not sure, but I think he was trying to suggest to you that all American corporations sell products that they know will kill and cripple people. He almost tried to make it sound like juries all over America every day hear about corporations that destroy documents, lie to the federal government, and publicly attack scientists who are critical of their dangerous products. Well, ladies and gentlemen, nothing could be farther from the truth. Most corporations in America have a respect for the law, or at least they should. They have a respect for human life, or at least they should. Most corporations don't engage in the caliber of cover-up and outright misinformation that you have seen with this company, or at least they should not.

Do you realize that you are six of the few people in America that will ever hear about what this company did? This is the first time these documents have ever been shown to a jury. You are the first jurors who will hear about this company's conduct. No, trials like this are actually very rare in America because most corporations are willing to conduct their business with an acceptable level of decency and concern for the people who buy their products, or at least they should.

### Opposing Counsel Ingratiates Himself with the Jurors

How do you handle closing argument when opposing counsel tries to ingratiate himself to a particular juror or group of jurors? Years ago, Fred Levin was trying a case against the L&N Railroad. His client had been killed as a result of what he contended was the negligence of the railroad. Opposing counsel was an outstanding trial lawyer who had been trying cases for substantially longer than Mr. Levin had lived. He was truly a great trial lawyer from the old school who tried cases in a way that relied much more on form than substance.

Things were going extremely well for Levin, and he was getting good jury reaction. The jury consisted of three white males, one white female, one African-American male, and one African-American female. There were also a couple of alternates. He was into the last week of trial when he noticed that opposing counsel, contrary to his past conduct during the trial, appeared in the courtroom before the jury came into the courtroom. Also, opposing counsel was surrounded by three or four black railroad employees who stood together with their arms around each other as if they were in a football huddle with opposing counsel being the quarterback. They remained in that "friendship huddle" until after the jury had come into the courtroom and had been seated for several minutes. The procedure at that time was for the jury to come in, and then approximately five minutes later the judge would enter the courtroom. Levin noticed that one of the gentlemen in the huddle had nodded an acknowledgment to the black male juror, as if he knew him. This went on every morning for the last week of trial. In closing argument, Mr. Levin said:

> The jury system as we know it in this country is the greatest system of justice in the world. However, the system only works if all of us who are involved in the system do what is expected. In other words, if the judge, the clerk, the court reporter, the lawyers, and most especially you, the jury, do what is expected, the system will work. But sometimes, there are those who would rather the system not work. We must be careful to avoid those situations. For example, many, many years ago, lawyers would try to curry favor with a jury by calling a juror by his name or being extremely cordial outside of the courtroom or things of that nature. That is the reason that His Honor, the judge, told you at the start of this case that the lawyers would not acknowledge you outside of this courtroom, and for you not to think of this as the lawyers being impolite or discourteous. There is a reason for this. There is a reason for jurors not to be influenced by anything other than the evidence and the law. I can remember when I first started practicing law, there was a trick that some of the older lawyers used to use that is a good example of what I just talked about. If there was a plumber on the jury, the old time lawyers would bring in another plumber who happened to be a friend of the juror and the lawyer would put his arm around the juror's friend.
>
> . . .

As Levin was arguing the above to the jury, the black male juror smiled at Levin with a look of "I understand and agree with exactly what you are saying." The case resulted in the largest wrongful death verdict in the history of the country as of that date.

## *Opposing Side Has the Eyewitnesses—And You Don't*

How do you respond to the situation where the eyewitnesses testify for the opposing side? The following is an example argument:

> The three eyewitnesses to this incident have all testified consistently and have all testified in favor of the defense. Are the three of them lying? Of course not. The problem is that they are trying to testify to something that occurred three years ago, and the only written document that exists to help refresh their recollection is the statement taken by the investigator for the defense.
>
> I am not suggesting that the investigator did not type the statements correctly, but the statements are virtually identical, and we all know that when ten people witness an incident, they always see it a little differently, and sometimes with major differences. Thus, the only way these statements could be identical is if the investigator was suggesting the answers through the form of his questioning. This is not to suggest that the investigator was doing anything wrong. It is simply a reality that the way a question is asked can affect the answer someone gives.
>
> This incident occurred in a split second. There was only a short period of time for the witnesses to see and hear everything and remember it. If the investigator asked the witness, "What color was the car that ran the red light?" the answer might be very different than if he asked the witness, "Did you see the blue car run the red light?" It has to do with the power of suggestion. In the first case, the witness may not recall that the car was blue, but in the second case, the investigator has suggested the answer and the witness may agree to this, thinking it is true.
>
> People have a desire to be helpful. They want to remember things. But once the person has stated in writing that he saw the

blue car run the red light, then forever afterwards he feels compelled to state or remember that the car was blue. He feels foolish if he changes his mind about what he saw or said. Similarly, if the investigator asks the witness whether the car was traveling between sixty and seventy miles per hour, the answer might be substantially different than if the investigator asks the witness what speed the car was traveling. In the first example, the investigator suggests to the witness that the speed must have been between sixty and seventy.

Suppose that I were to give each of you jurors a questionnaire and ask you about something that occurred in this courtroom in the last twenty minutes. If I were to ask you specific things about what the judge was doing several minutes ago; whether he was reading something or writing something, or had removed his glasses, or for that matter, how many light fixtures there are about you, or without looking, tell me what the color of the seat that you're sitting in is, etc., etc., I'm sure we'd probably get two or three different answers among the six of you.

Unfortunately, those are the types of problems that always arise with eyewitness testimony. That is why the judge told you that you were not supposed to consider a decision in the case until you heard all parts of all the pieces you must fit together to arrive at a decision in this case.

This is why physical evidence, common sense, and logic are much more important than witness recollection when determining the truth of the situation. What does the physical evidence and common sense show in this case?

. . .

### *The Law Appears to Be Unconscionable or Illogical*

As stated many times, jurors want to do the right thing. Sometimes, however, the law does not appear reasonable or logical, and the jury has a difficult time applying the law. How do you handle this situation? The following is a recommended response:

> When we were picking you to serve on this jury, several of you disagreed with the law that imposes on the defendant responsibility for the death of this sixteen-year-old girl. To some of you, it just doesn't seem fair that this little girl could come in and buy alcohol, get drunk, and go out and drive her vehicle off the road, and the parents sue the bar for the child's death. I wouldn't doubt that when you, as a jury, retire to the jury room, at least one of you is going to say, "It just doesn't seem fair." That same juror might go on to say, "What would be wrong if just this time we did not apply the law because the law just isn't fair?"
>
> Our country is the greatest country in the world, and our legal system is the envy of every other country in the world. The basic reason is that we are a government of laws, not of men. We cannot, as a jury, decide to apply those laws that we like and not apply those laws that we don't like.
>
> I want to tell you a story that Professor Day told my law school class many, many years ago in order to explain the concept that we are now discussing. Professor Day had been teaching law school for probably fifty years, and this was the last year before his retirement. He asked all of us law students the exact question that I just asked you: "If a law seems wrong to me, why should I have to follow it?" Professor Day answered it like this:
>
>> I was born in a little Alabama town ten years after the Civil War ended. My father was the Circuit Judge, which meant

that he rode the circuit. That is, he went from town to town to dispense justice and hold Court. There came a time that I was leaving high school and going to study law. I was going to study law in Birmingham and at the same time to clerk for one of my father's friends who was a Circuit Judge in Birmingham. Before I left, my father took me to the town square in my hometown. He told me that he was going to show me why our system of justice was the greatest in the world. He said it is because we are a government of laws. It's because we cannot survive with each person deciding only to follow those laws that the person considers to be good.

As we were walking in the town square, he looked up at the clock that was on top of City Hall. He asked me whether I realized that in virtually every community the clock that controlled the town was way up high and usually on the top of the City Hall. Why would the clock be up there rather than at eye level on the street? He went on to tell me, imagine the chaos if the town clock were at eye level. He said that Mr. Brown would be walking down the sidewalk and look over at the clock and see that it said 2:15. Mr. Brown would look at his pocket watch and see that it says 2:10. He would then reach over to the town clock and change it from 2:15 to 2:10. A few minutes later, Mr. Smith would walk by, and he would see that the clock said 2:10, and when he would look at his pocket watch, it might show 2:20. Mr. Smith would then change the town clock from 2:10 to 2:20, and so on and so on. However, when the town clock is way up high, both Mr. Brown and Mr. Smith would change their watches so that they would be consistent with the town clock, and everyone in the community would always be guided by the same time schedule. Regardless of whether the town clock was right or wrong, when everyone followed it, we were able to survive as a community.

That is the reason we are such a great country, because we try as best we can to make certain the laws are fair and just. But even if the laws in our mind are not always fair and just, and even if the clock is ten minutes off; as long as we all go by the same clock, we are going to come to work at the same time, go to lunch at the same time, and get off at the same time. It is only when the clock is at eye level, and we can change it to fit what we think is the right time that we become no better than those countries that are governed by the whim of one or more persons and not by a law that applies equally.

### The Vindictive Juror

The great majority of jurors truly believe in their oath and want to do what the law provides. If you come across a potential juror who does not feel this way, you obviously should get rid of him during the voir dire. But what if one gets by you, and you learn about that bias during the presentation of your case? It may become obvious because you learn some fact about the juror that you missed during voir dire. Or perhaps what you observe, what you hear, what you instinctively figure out during trial leads you to believe that a particular juror is hopelessly biased against you and your client. As with everything in the practice of trial law, the best answer to a problem like this is to bring the problem to the surface by talking about it. Hiding from the obvious will never make things better.

Several years ago, one of the authors was trying a medical malpractice case with a young lawyer in our firm. A female juror during voir dire had answered all of the voir dire questions as if she would be the perfect plaintiff's juror. The truth is that she was extremely hostile toward our firm but remained silent about her hostility because she believed she could vent her hostility by helping to bring about an adverse verdict against our client. Three or four events occurred during trial that brought her previously well-concealed hostility to the surface. As the trial progressed, one of our partners happened to recall this person and remembered that he had represented her husband in a child custody action probably twenty-five years in the past. Her name had failed to show up on our jury pool data check because the custody action had occurred so many years before. We pulled the file and found out that we had successfully represented the husband in the child custody action and taken this juror's only child away. We immediately had the voir dire examination typed and found that the young lawyer in our firm had failed to ask a question in voir dire that would have specifically brought out the fact that we had been on the other side twenty-five years before.

The first thing we did was to call this to the Court's attention and to have His Honor question the juror outside the presence of any of the attorneys. The juror convinced the judge that she would be totally fair. We were left with only argument as a way to minimize the damage that this one juror could cause our client. Here is the argument that we directed clearly at her:

Our system of justice works only when each juror accepts the obligations that he or she has sworn to uphold during the juror oath. The system doesn't work if one or more jurors refuse to abide by the oath. Every once in a while, for any of a hundred different reasons, a juror decides that in this case he or she has a personal agenda. The juror knows what's right and what's wrong, but because of a personal reason, he or she wants to use the trial as "payback time." Whenever a juror begins to feel this way, he or she needs to sincerely think of what he or she is doing and the consequences. This case involves real lives and real people. This is the one and only decision for my client. What you do in your verdict is forever. It is permanent. My client does not get a second chance before another jury. It is over. There is also no chance at a later time for a juror to say, "I did wrong. I hurt the client who was an innocent victim of my anger." There is no way at a later time to make it right. The decision you make today is a decision you need to be proud about because it is a decision you will live with for the remainder of your life. If there is something that has caused you anger, there are other ways and will be other times to address that anger in the right way.

This obviously is the type of argument that should be delivered as a proverbial "last resort." But once the decision is made, the argument must be directed to the juror with very clear eye contact. It must be obvious to the rest of the jurors that perhaps this juror has been untruthful and that her memory, observations, and opinions about the facts of the case might be tainted and unreliable during jury deliberation. Further, it might cause jurors to ask her why such an argument was directed toward her.

### When a Judge Becomes Capricious

There are few trial lawyers who have not been confronted by a trial judge who decides that his personal beliefs conflict with the law and who therefore becomes unwilling to preside as a fair and impartial judge. These are the types of judges who in the course of a trial become shameless about the way they attempt to stack the deck against you and your client. Most of the time the problem is not that the judge does not have the judicial talent and sophistication to preside in a way that comports with the law. Unfortunately, it is more often a situation where the judge does not have the wisdom, or character, or courage, to overcome his bias.

We had exactly that experience with a judge in Nashville, Tennessee. The facts in that case were as follows:

The plaintiff was a truck driver who was hauling gravel from a gravel pit to be loaded on freight cars, a distance of approximately two miles. In order to get the gravel to the freight cars, the driver had to cross a railroad crossing that was controlled by flashing lights. Approximately half the time, however, the flashing lights would flash when there was no train approaching, and this truck driver was well aware of this fact, having crossed the crossing over 300 times in a one-month period. At the time of the accident, the truck driver had come up to the crossing and stopped for the flashing lights and did not see an approaching train. He then proceeded to cross, but a speeding train came through and caused very serious brain damage to the driver. Under the law of Tennessee, contributory negligence was a complete bar to recovery.

We were before a federal judge in Nashville, and we were suing the Louisville and Nashville Railroad. It was clear at the pre-trial conference that the judge did not like our case. On the other side was the L&N Railroad, which was represented by the most prestigious and political firms in Tennessee. The judge was a Carter Democrat appointee. One of the defense firms had been instrumental in helping with that appointment. The defense filed a motion in limine that we should not be allowed to show that the flashing lights would flash half the time when no train was approaching. Of course, we never dreamed this would be granted, as this was the key fact on the issue of contributory negligence and negligence. It was a fact that went to the heart of the case.

During the week leading up to trial, we had three or four hearings before the judge. The judge kept avoiding the issue even though he clearly understood the critical nature of the testimony. Five minutes before we were to stand and make opening statement, the judge turned to us and stated he was granting the motion and that we were not to mention that the crossing lights often flashed when there was no train approaching, and consequently, we had little explanation as to why the truck driver proceeded through the flashing lights. The judge's overt animosity toward us and our client continued to grow throughout trial. When we put an expert on the stand, the judge would pick up a newspaper and turn his back on our witness. When the defense put an expert on the stand, the judge would actually get up from the bench and stand next to the witness while the defense witness testified. Of course, he would smile and grimace at the appropriate places during the witness testimony.

There are times when the conduct of the trial judge becomes so extraordinarily offensive to the democratic process that your only choice is to address the problem in an extraordinary fashion. Here is an argument that is, in our opinion, appropriate to address the type of judicial conduct described above:

A trial is somewhat like a football game. The lawyers are like the coaches. The judge is like the referee who is supposed to make sure the game is played fair. The jury keeps the score, and determines who wins. One way I can describe it for you is like this:

I'm a big University of Florida football fan. Last year I went to watch the Gators play Alabama at Florida Field, where the Gators had not lost a home game in many years. But on that day, one of the running backs for Alabama, whose name I believe was Shaun Alexander, completely rolled over the Gators and probably gained more than 200 yards. Every time Shaun would break loose for a long gain, I was hopeful that the referee had thrown a flag.

But even as an avid fan, I wonder how I would have felt if every time Shaun broke loose, the referee threw an unwarranted flag? It would finally reach a point that I would have realized we were not playing fair because the referee was not objective. And somehow I believe that even the most avid fan would not stand for this. Even the most avid fan would see the line between what's fair and what's not fair.

What does this story have to do with a courtroom and a jury? Sometimes, the jury understands a lot more than we realize. Sometimes, if things get out of hand, it's up to the scorekeepers to level the playing field. Each of us in a courtroom has certain obligations. That includes the judge, the lawyers, the court reporter, and the jury. Lawyers have an obligation to be totally respectful of the system, the court, and the judge. If we become disrespectful, we can be held in contempt and thrown in jail. The jury has an obligation to do the right thing even if that decision might be contrary to what the community thinks, contrary to what the lawyers think, and you know what? Even if it is contrary to what the judge thinks.

The reason juries can do this is because there is nothing that can be done to a jury for the decision it returns. In fact, in America, our democratic process only works because juries have the extraordinary, unquestionable right to have the last word in a trial like this even if the last word is different from the personal wishes of the parties, the lawyers, and the judge who sits as a referee. That is an exceptional amount of power. I hope you will use that power in a way that ensures that this trial is a fair fight...in a way that sustains a level playing field. This is not a game. You do what you know is justice.

### *"Reasonable Man" Standard*

A popular approach for defense lawyers in arguing the reasonableness of their client's conduct is to emphasize and re-emphasize the obvious truth that "no one is perfect." Their focus is typically that the law does not require that their client do everything perfectly, but simply that their client acts as "reasonably" as the jurors would act under similar circumstances. Another way of selling this concept is to suggest that the law does not require a grade of "A" all of the time. Instead, a "B" or even a "C" grade is the best that most people can hope for in the way they conduct their lives day-to-day, and "that is all that common sense and the law requires."

One can consider the following argument to counter this defense theme:

> For over 200 years, the law has been developing ways for jurors like yourselves to gauge what is reasonable or unreasonable conduct when people interact together in a community, as neighbors. If we were to grade our day-to-day actions, we would all make more C's than A's, and that is a good thing. It simply means that we are all human and we all make errors. But whether our everyday actions are worthy of a grade of "A" or "C" is a far different issue than whether a specific action is right or wrong. The question is not whether we would give Mr. Jones an "A" or a "C" in what he did that day. The question is whether everyday people would know that driving a car 55 m.p.h. in a 35 m.p.h. speed zone is wrong, and the consequences are that someone could likely get hurt. The issue is not whether other people do it, because other people might also be wrong. What matters is whether Mr. Jones was on notice that if something did go wrong because of his actions that he was going to be held responsible in a court of law. There is no doubt Mr. Jones knew this because it is common sense. It is common sense that when you drive 55 m.p.h. in a 35 m.p.h. speed zone that you are driving negligently and that under the law you should be held responsible for your actions.

### Anyone Can Bring a Lawsuit

If you have not heard the words come out of a defense lawyer's mouth declaring, "anyone and everyone can initiate a lawsuit," then you probably have not been to trial in the last five years. Generally, it is first heard in voir dire, then repeated in opening, and then once again stated in closing. You have to be prepared to deal with it. Here is a suggested concept of turning it around and making it part of the theme for your argument:

> I have heard Lawyer Smith tell us not less than a dozen times in this trial that "anyone can bring a lawsuit." That all a person has to do is draw up the right papers, and we end up in a courtroom like this, arguing to jurors like you. I am pretty comfortable with the fact that you know that is not true. Yes, any person can file a lawsuit, but not any person can appear before a jury. This is because the defense has the ability to file motions to get baseless lawsuits dismissed, and judges can dismiss baseless lawsuits before they get to a jury.
>
> Mrs. Bowers is here before you, the jury, not because she could file a lawsuit. She is here because XYZ Corporation made a product that is so dangerous that it is has been pulled from the market.
>
> Mrs. Bowers is here before you, the jury, because XYZ Corporation has an established track record of making a product that is purely about profit and not really about helping anyone.
>
> Mrs. Bowers is here before you, the jury, because her lawyers and staff have spent years investigating this case—experts flying in from all over the country—doctors testifying—scientists testifying. Is counsel for XYZ Corporation suggesting that this type of case goes on everyday around here, or is counsel simply trying to trivialize the magnitude of the harm and injury his client has

caused? Fortunately, our civil justice system is such that you are the judge. The truth is, people like Mrs. Bowers bring lawsuits only when it is their last alternative.

## *Burden of Proof*

An experienced defense lawyer will typically take the burden of proof standard that is required in a plaintiff's case and make that standard appear virtually impossible to reach. They will make it appear that a plaintiff actually meeting that standard is rare as a solar eclipse. Your goal as a plaintiff's lawyer should explain it as simply and concisely as possible.

Ladies and gentlemen: The judge is going to talk to you about the standards that we must meet in this case in order to win. Fortunately, that standard is very easy to follow. You will hear that we have the burden of proof by the "greater weight of the evidence." What does this mean? I like to look at it like the scales of justice. On one side of the scale is our evidence; on the other side is their evidence. Which side weighs more? If I were to take this one tiny little rock out of my pocket and put it on the scale, and it tipped the scale our direction even a fraction; then the greater weight of the evidence is on our side, and your verdict should be for my client, Ms. Jones.

We do not have the burden to prove anything beyond a reasonable doubt. "Beyond a reasonable doubt" is the test in a criminal case. In a criminal case, you must prove your case beyond and to the exclusion of every reasonable doubt. That's not the test here because this is not a criminal case; and no matter what you do, no matter how much you find in your verdict for damages in this case, nobody is going to go to jail. Nobody is going to lose his job, and nobody is going to receive a fine.

Your job is to determine what is the more likely scenario, and that's who wins. A case is like a jigsaw puzzle. Once you get enough pieces, you know what the puzzle is. We can't sit here and put on every piece of the puzzle. We would be here for weeks and months and years. Mr. [Defense Counsel] and I have lived with this case for many years. We know more about this case than anyone else could possibly know. If there was any evidence that would have been beneficial to either side, you would have seen it. Don't go back and start thinking, "Well, we didn't see this," or "I don't know this," or start saying, "Well, I know about this." Rely upon the evidence because things that you might think, might not be correct, and we do not have a chance to discuss it with you. We don't have a chance to argue it. We don't have a chance to go back to our files and say, "Look, we've got something on that." We just can't do that.

The jury instructions that you will hear read by the judge allow for you to have some element of doubt in your mind about parts of this case and still find in favor of my client. The real question that you have to answer is, "Which side's evidence tips the scales of justice ever the slightest amount?"

### Contributory Negligence

Far too many cases have been lost for plaintiffs when a good defense lawyer has made contributory negligence the single focus of the defense while the plaintiff's lawyer ignores the defense and hopes the jury simply will forgive it and forget it. If you are trying cases in one of the less progressive contributory negligence jurisdictions, you absolutely must have a broad collection of well-practiced arguments that confront the problem head-on. The following is just one suggestion:

As I was watching the way [Mr. Defense Lawyer] was trying this case, it was pretty obvious what he was asking you as a jury to do.

He was hoping that you would hold Mrs. Bass to an impossible standard of being "a perfect human being;" a person with absolute perfect judgment, perfect luck, perfect in every way. Hard as we try, that is a standard that very few of us are able to live up to, and I really do admire this defense lawyer for his effort to try. But as far as the actual law in this case is concerned, there is no perfect human judgment, no perfect human standard that we are expected or required to reach in this case.

When counsel for the defense started talking about this principle that is referred to as contributory negligence in his opening statement at the beginning of this trial, he almost made it sound like my client, Mrs. Bass, should not recover anything for her injuries, for her suffering. He made it sound like Mrs. Bass was somehow responsible for the defendant driving seventy miles per hour and crashing into the side of her car. There is no question that Mrs. Bass' judgment and decision making were not as good as they should have been in avoiding this accident. But the law does not require her to make a score of 100 every time she is called upon to make a quick decision, or a snap judgment—a pop quiz. If we were tested and graded every time we had to make the kind of decision Mrs. Bass had to make that day, the best grade that most of us could hope for on the defense counsel's grading scale might be a 70 or an 80, maybe a 90, but that still would mean that we failed this defense lawyer's test. It still would not mean that the defendant in this case should walk out of this courtroom without paying a dime for all the suffering he has caused. Ladies and gentlemen: We simply are not required to make a grade of 100 ever time we use our best judgment. The law does not require it, and justice does not require it. All that justice requires is that Mrs. Bass acted reasonably in light of the horrendous conduct of the defendant when Mrs. Bass only a split second to react.

### *When the Adverse Expert Witness Hurts Your Case*

Like it or not, the best of cross-examiners will sometimes get hurt by the testimony of a talented highly compensated expert witness. The case is far from over simply because your theory gets burned down by such a witness. But the key to resurrecting your theory is to have a good plan during closing arguments.

When an adverse expert witness hammers your case in trial, one age-old plan of attack is to try to neutralize the importance of all the expert witness testimony on both sides and argue the importance of common sense. The following is one example of such an approach:

> The beauty of the jury system is that people such as yourselves get to sit as judges of the facts. A jury is made up of people who have learned more about life through experience, mistakes, successes, pain, and pleasure than can ever be learned with doctoral degrees. Real life is always a better teacher than academic life.

> Both sides in this case paid their experts over $50,000 each to come in here and testify. Each expert got paid more in one case than most people make in two years of working. The experts came in here to tell us that by applying complicated scientific and mathematical analysis they can prove their side is the correct position, even though both experts reach totally opposite conclusions. The experts said their opinions were not influenced at all by the $50,000 being paid to them by the lawyer calling them to the stand. Real-life experience tells you this isn't true.

> So what do you do when you are not sure about the expert testimony because of bias? You do what is the most important thing to do when making any decision. You use your common sense. What does common sense say in this case? Let's look at the facts from the unbiased evidence and witnesses.

. . .

When I brought Dr. Phelps into court to give his opinions about what happened in this case, I never expected you to go back into the jury room and accept everything he said as being the absolute answers to all the important questions in this case. In fact, I understand after many years of trying cases that most of the time juries place very little importance on the testimony of experts. Most of the time, they use their common sense to reach decisions in cases, which is the correct way to reach your decision. In fact, as you will hear from the judge, the law tells you that when judging the credibility of any witness, including an expert witness, you judge that witness in light of your own experience and common sense. That instruction is there because the law recognizes that your collective common sense, your life experience as jurors, does not flow from the ivory towers that both Dr. Phelps and Dr. Morris spend all day in, theorizing, speculating, and sometimes simply guessing about how the world works. The law recognizes that you as jurors in your collective wisdom and real-world experience have the ability to figure out tough problems far better than Dr. Phelps or Dr. Morris.

The bottom line is that an expert witness is a paid actor. He comes into a courtroom to perform and to convince you that the position of the attorney calling him is the correct position. If an expert witness does not agree with the position of the attorney calling him, then the attorney obviously would not hire him, and the expert would lose a large source of income. This is why you have the right to disregard all of the expert testimony, including my experts, and to rely upon your common sense and the evidence presented.

## *Negligence*

Far too many words are spoken by lawyers trying to sell the concept of negligence during their closing statement. The concept of "keep it simple, stupid" is more important during closing argument than most other parts of the trial. Because of that, an explanation of negligence should only touch on very basic concepts: (1) nobody performed an intentional act, and we do not have to show that it was intentional; (2) someone did something or failed to do something that any person with reasonable common sense would not do; and (3) because someone did or failed to do something, our client was hurt. Keep lawyer talk to an absolute minimum when you attempt to explain negligence.

> Ladies and gentlemen: You have heard lawyers and witnesses and even the judge use the term "negligence" in the course of this trial. It is a term you will have to talk about back in the jury room. Fortunately, the term "negligence" is no different in a legal setting such as a trial than it is when you use it in every other part of your life. The question is whether someone dropped the ball by doing something that most people with a normal amount of common sense would not do? For example, does it seem like good common sense for a company that is in the business of manufacturing drugs to sell a drug without even testing it? Or did the company fail to use common sense? My grandfather used to hit the nail on the head about what negligence was when I would show bad judgment and do something or fail to do something that could hurt someone. He would tell me that sometimes I don't show good walking-around sense. He didn't know the legal definition of negligence, but he knew what it looked like.

## Comparative Negligence

Never assume that the jury understands how the application of comparative negligence will affect your client's final award of damages. Take a few minutes to explain that the way they divide up percentages of negligence between your client and the defendant really does matter.

> Mr. [Defense Counsel] has spent a great deal of time in this trial focusing on what he believed Mrs. Baker did wrong, almost as if Mrs. Baker were responsible for her injuries. Well, let's assume that for some reason you assign a percentage of negligence to Mrs. Baker even though it was the defendant who ran the stop sign. If you do what the defendant's lawyer wants you to do and say that Mrs. Baker was 40 percent responsible for her injuries, then you are saying that the defendant is only 60 percent responsible. If the defendant is only 60 percent negligent, then Mrs. Baker only receives 60 percent of her medical expenses, wage loss, and pain and suffering, even though she suffered 100 percent of her medical expenses, wage loss, and pain and suffering. For example, if you truly believe that Mrs. Baker has suffered medical expenses, wage loss, and pain and suffering in the amount of $100,000; but you find the defendant only 60 percent responsible, then Mrs. Baker only receives $60,000. Would this really be justice under the facts of this case?

## Damages: Explaining the Philosophy

Now, more than ever, it is imperative that you make the jury feel good about the decision to make a large damage award in your case. Do not assume that corporate America's well-orchestrated jury contamination campaign has been successful to the point that a jury will not hammer a culpable defendant in most cases. Empirical data shows that a jury will. However, it is critical that you take the time somewhere in your closing to explain to jurors where the concept of money damages originated.

Explain to the jury why money damages are such a common sense solution to conflict between two parties:

> A little more than 200 years ago, Mr. Baxter, my client, would have had the legal right to challenge Mr. DeVink, the CEO of this big corporation, to a duel to the death because of how the actions of Mr. DeVink played into the death of Mr. Baxter's wife. Mr. Baxter could have picked a time and a place for the duel. Referees and judges to oversee the gun duel would have been present, and either Mr. Baxter or Mr. DeVink would lie dead on the ground by the time that duel was over. The stakes were very high in the way two people would deal with disputes such as the one we have heard about in this trial this week. People would simply take civil disputes into their own hands and let the chips fall as they might.
>
> Well, in America, lawmakers decided that there needed to be a better way for two people to resolve their disputes. The civil jury system is now the only legal way available for a man like Mr. Baxter to confront a man like Mr. DeVink. Not by violence with a sword, but by the wisdom and insight of a jury.

### The Role of Juries

Too often, a trial lawyer will move through a two- or three-week trial and talk to a jury about its role only at the voir dire stage of the trial. Often a lawyer will spend too much time trying to analyze what a nod or a yawn or a snicker from a juror means. That time could be better spent paying attention to better educating jurors about what their role in the trial should be. We occasionally forget that most jurors do not have a clue about what the civil justice system expects of them because the jury instructions typically do not read well and are not particularly easy to follow when read aloud by most judges. The various roles of the jury should be stated, restated, and then stated again as often as possible from the time the trial begins until the end of closing. Below are a variety of ideas about jurors' roles that should be emphasized throughout the trial according to how they are needed in a particular fact situation:

- Their role is one of service that holds all the parts of democracy together. It is only through their service that the greatest judicial system in the world can exist.

- Their role is not to act like a legislator or politician and change the law according to how they think it should be but to follow the law as it is.

- Their role is to do what is sometimes almost impossible to do, which is to abandon their prejudices, biases, angry attitudes, and cynicism and replace all those negative human emotions with the wisdom, understanding, forgiveness, and compassion of Solomon.

- Their role is to accept the huge responsibility they agreed to in voir dire. That responsibility is to correct the injustice that we have seen from the facts of this case. This is no time to run from that huge responsibility. This is their time to roll up their sleeves and accept that responsibility.

- Their role is to do what may be uncommon in their everyday life. They are now confronted with having to make the kinds of choices and decisions that might be uncommon day-to-day for most of us. Those uncommon decisions require uncommon honesty and uncommon character.

- Their role is to understand the breadth of their power. They need to be willing to understand that their power to fix things in this trial is greater than that of any politician, any lawyer, even any judge as long as they use that incredible amount of power according to the law of this state.

- Their role is to remember a little bit of history about how many wars have been fought and how huge the price has been that allows them to sit as decision makers in a trial that takes place in America's democracy. History shows that it is the greatest civil justice system in the world.

- Their role is relying on the common sense that they have developed in their years on this earth. They must not be afraid to draw on the collective common sense that they rely on everyday to evaluate and solve problems. When expert witness testimony differs from their common sense, they are probably better off with their own instinct and insight about how the world works.

- Their role is to evaluate and weigh only the evidence that has been presented in the trial. When they are back in the jury room deliberating, if one of them suggests that he knows about some fact or information about the incident that was not made part of this evidence, then it is their duty to remind him that that information cannot be considered. Their role is not to play Perry Mason or Sherlock Holmes and speculate about what evidence could or should have been presented. Their role is to merely weigh the evidence that was actually presented in this case on this day.

- Their role is not to try to dominate the discussion back in the jury room. It makes more sense to allow an open-minded discussion to take place. The deliberation should be respectful. Too often we see television shows these days where everyone on the show wants to believe that they are the expert and they have all the answers. They yell and they scream. They fail to listen to what the other participants have to say. They fail to honor the feelings and insight of people with whom they disagree.

- It is their role to now carry on the burden that has been passed to them. The judge has carried his burden. The lawyers have attempted to shoulder their burden. And now that burden has been shifted to the shoulders of the jury.

- Their role is to use their own sense of fairness where it comes to damage awards. What one lawyer said might sound like too much money for a damage award. What the other lawyer said may not sound like enough. We have to draw on our own common sense of decency and fairness everyday. Today is no different.

- Their role is one that deserves a sense of gratitude and thanks from your client. If it were not for jurors like them who were willing to take the time to work hard to be fair, unbiased, attentive, to struggle with all these facts, the system would not work. If it were not for jurors like them who were willing to serve democracy, then your client would be subject to being judged by bureaucrats and politicians as occurs in so many other countries around the world. Your client would not be judged by her peers. Instead, it would be justice by committee. The kind of justice that takes place in Russia, Iraq, or Red China. So they all are deserving of our sincere thanks for their time here this week.

- It is their role to be willing to take their time in deliberation and not feel rushed or pushed. It is their role to give this case the time it deserves in deliberation because this will be positively, absolutely the only time that your client will have his day in court. They will not be able to return next week or next month and have this case heard again. The time this jury takes this week will be the last time that is ever devoted to having justice done. It has taken your client three years from the time she first filed this case to have these few days to tell her story to jurors.

- Their role is to understand that juries affect important powerful change in America. When corporations do wrong, when the government does wrong, it is only the jury system in America that

79

can make all of that right. Because of juries, we have safer cars, safer pharmaceuticals, safer schools, safer nursing homes. Juries have done more than all the politicians and bureaucrats put together where it comes to protecting the safety and rights of Americans.

- It is their role to avoid making this a popularity contest between the lawyers. All of them understand that Mr. [Defense Lawyer] is only the lawyer for this corporation. He did not make the decisions that have put this corporation in this courtroom. Obviously, they chose Mr. [Defense Lawyer] because he is a capable, likeable, charismatic character who can put the most positive face on this corporation, but this corporation must understand that this trial is not like a game show, or a television miniseries, or a popularity contest. This case is a real life tragedy for your client. And wouldn't it be a terrible disservice to our system if they went back into that jury room and made their decisions according to how much they liked or disliked the lawyer that this corporation is paying to put the best face on their case? Wouldn't that be a shallow, hollow way for justice to take place in America?

- It is their role to understand that they have not been called upon to show vengeance or forgiveness where it comes to judging the actions of this corporation. There is little question that the way the witnesses for this corporation testified made it sound as if they were asking for forgiveness. Almost as if you the jury will forgive them this time, this will never happen again, but the law does not expect the jury to figure out when and if the jury should forgive and forget. The law only expects the jury to sort through the facts, weigh the evidence, use its common sense and reach a decision based on those things alone. Your client is not entitled to the jury's sympathy, just as the defendant is not entitled to the jury's forgiveness.

## Chapter 5
## AREAS TO ADDRESS IN THE
## REBUTTAL PORTION OF CLOSING

### *The Defendant Made a Mistake. He Did Not Intend the Harm.*

In many civil cases, defense counsel will argue that the defendant should not be liable because he simply "made a mistake" or "it was only an accident." We address this argument as follows:

> The defense counsel keeps saying that this was all an accident, and that no one was negligent. I would like you to ask yourself a question. What if the defendant had been driving a car and because he was thinking about something else he failed to notice a stop sign and caused a collision? No one would say that the defendant intended to run the stop sign, nor did he intend to hurt anyone. However, he clearly made a mistake. He should have been more cautious considering the consequences of running the stop sign. This is what negligence is all about, and this is what makes a civil case different from a criminal case. In a civil case like this one, no one goes to jail. The law does not require us to prove that the defendant intended to do something or that he meant to hurt someone. The law says that we only must prove that he failed to act reasonably under the circumstances.

## *The Accident and Injury Was Merely "Fate"*

The defense has argued or inferred "it was fate that caused Billy to die in this accident" or "we cannot determine at this time why bad things happen to good people, but someday we will." How do you handle this argument?

Any attempt to inject God or religion into a trial is not proper, and is beyond the bounds of trial advocacy. However, religious-oriented arguments strongly appeal to some jurors. If you have one or more jurors who believe that everything is preordained, opposing counsel's insinuation that the accident and injury were fate is extremely convincing.

If opposing counsel makes an argument that touches on this, you must assume that there are jurors who will find the argument convincing. Therefore, you cannot argue that there is no such thing as fate or that this accident and injuries were not preordained. We suggest something such as the following:

> Counsel has stated that we do not know why this accident happened or why my client was so seriously injured. He argues that maybe someday we will understand why horrible things happen to good people. I cannot answer the question whether everything in life is preordained or whether we have control over some aspects of our life. I do not know if it was preordained that the defendant was going to run this stop sign and cause my client to become a paraplegic, or whether my client was simply unfortunate to be where he was at the time the defendant chose to run the stop sign. But if Mr. Smith is correct, and it was preordained that this incident was going to happen, then there seems to be some preordained justice in the fact that this accident occurred in Florida where the law of damages provides for full and fair compensation when someone is seriously injured because of the fault of another. Likewise, it must have been

preordained that out of all the persons living in this county called for jury duty, each of you was chosen to sit on this jury, and each of you took an oath that you would follow the Court's instructions on Florida law and award full and fair compensation.

Having said all this, let's talk again about the facts of this case...

### Plaintiff "Is in a Better Place" Argument

Similar to the "fate" argument, defense counsel will sometimes argue to the jury that it should not award the survivors in a wrongful death case any significant money because the deceased was a devout Christian and now "is in a better place." While this type of argument is extremely improper, and possibly reversible error, the authors have seen the argument effectively presented. When faced with this argument, we suggest responding as follows:

Defense counsel argues that Mr. and Mrs. Smith were devout Christians, and hence Mrs. Smith is now in a much better place, and Mr. Smith should not seek nor be entitled to significant money damages because his faith in the Lord should be enough to sustain him. Basically, what defense counsel is stating is that Mr. and Mrs. Smith should be treated differently under the law because of their religious beliefs. This is an improper argument and is against the oath you took as jurors. We do not treat people differently because of race, religion, nationality, gender, or wealth. Defense counsel says to treat Mr. and Mrs. Smith differently because they were devout Christians. Do not award them the same amount of money you would award another person who is not as strongly religious. Is defense counsel saying that the less religious a person is, then the more money they should be awarded? That does not make sense. Religion should have no place in a decision regarding the value of what Mr.

Smith has lost. If we accept the defense argument at face value, then it means that someone who leads a life of hatred and violence has a case in a courtroom in America that is worth substantially more money than someone who has lived a life of generosity and kindness. That is what my opposing counsel has just suggested to you with a straight face. That cannot be the law and that cannot be justice.

### The Doctor Did His Best to Help the Plaintiff

In a medical malpractice trial, we often hear defense counsel explain to the jury the Hippocratic Oath and how the doctor did everything he could to help the plaintiff, who is so unappreciative that he is suing the person who tried to help him. As this is being argued, the defendant doctor will lower his head and look toward the jury with soulful eyes. When this is argued, we suggest responding as follows:

> In the book *Of Mice and Men*, John Steinbeck tells the story of two close friends. One was named Lenny, and the other was named George. Lenny was an extremely trusting, caring, and giving individual, but he was mentally slow. George was very smart and clever and a very caring friend. George was always playing well-meaning jokes on Lenny, but one day, those well-meaning jokes almost cost Lenny his life.
>
> George would never dream of intentionally hurting Lenny. Lenny was a friend, but on this day, George and Lenny were fishing on the edge of a lake when George told Lenny that he should jump into the lake and go to the bottom and see if there were any fish to catch. George was doing this only as a friendly, well-meaning joke, but Lenny, because of his slow mind, was at a disadvantage and always did everything George told him to do. The only problem here is that George's well-meaning, friendly joke almost caused Lenny to drown because Lenny could not

swim. He simply had blind, unquestioning, unwavering faith and belief in George. He jumped into the deep water because he believed in George. He never dreamed that George could cause him any harm.

That day, George jumped into the lake and saved Lenny's life. Ever since that day, Lenny has told all his friends how proud he was of his hero, his best friend George for jumping in the lake and saving his life. Lenny did not understand in his naïve, childlike, trusting mind that it was George who caused Lenny the harm by having him jump into the lake when Lenny could not swim.

As defense counsel stood before you a few minutes ago telling you that Mr. Smith should be thanking Dr. Jones for what Dr. Jones did, and not suing Dr. Jones, I can't help but think of George and Lenny. In this case, it was Dr. Jones who caused this harm to Mr. Smith. It was Mr. Smith who trusted and believed in Dr. Jones. It is Dr. Jones who almost cost Mr. Smith his life. And now, it is Dr. Jones who wants Mr. Smith and the rest of the world to believe that Dr. Jones is a hero.

### *Opposing Side Presents an Absurd and Insulting Case*

Sometimes the opposing side presents what is obviously an absurd and insulting case. While the opposing side knows the probability of succeeding is low, there is always a chance. Thus, the opposing side perceives no harm in attempting to "pull the wool over the eyes of the jurors." At times opposing counsel may present ridiculous theories, and other times the clients might outright lie. When this occurs, you might consider something similar to the following at the very end of your argument, and if representing the plaintiff, at the end of the rebuttal argument. However, you first must carefully review your state's law on closing argument to make sure the following argument is not error, as some courts have found this type of argument reversible.

I want to close by commenting on the defendant's testimony in this case. If you believe the testimony presented by the defendant is unbelievable and ridiculous, then you have to consider why he would say this. There could be only one reason, and that is that he hoped you would believe it. He is willing to say and do anything on the slim chance that you, the jury, might find in his favor. Truth and justice is nowhere near as important as victory.

It is understandable why the defendant would attempt to present such an unbelievable story when faced with the overwhelming facts of this case, but it is wrong. A courtroom is supposed to be a place for the search for the truth and for justice. It is not a place for games. The defense's action in this case is insulting to everyone in this courtroom, and especially to the judicial system.

Picture the statue of the Lady of Justice. She has the sword in one hand to demonstrate the power of the law. She has the scales of justice in the other hand to demonstrate the balance of justice. Most important, she is always blindfolded. She is blindfolded because when she administers justice, she cannot see a person's race, gender, religion, nationality, or wealth.

Standing here and thinking about the testimony and arguments that have been presented by the defendant, it makes you wonder if the blindfold has another purpose in this case. I believe if we were to lift up the blindfold of our Lady of Justice, you would see that it was covering a tear—a tear of shame for what occurred here in this courtroom this week.

### *Future Economic Damages Are "Ridiculous"*

How do you handle the defense counsel argument that plaintiff counsel's economist has presented ridiculous testimony? For example, how should you respond to the argument by defense counsel that if the jury believes plaintiff's economic expert, then the jury has to believe that fifty years from now a doctor's visit will cost $20,000 per visit.

The above is just one of the many "cheap shots" that opposing counsel might take. In other words, there are times when an attorney knows what the truth is, but the attorney also knows the truth sounds strange. For example, if physician care has been historically rising by 9% per year, then the cost of a physician visit will double every 8 years. If a physician visit costs $300 per exam today, then in 48 years the cost will have doubled six times, and will be approximately $20,000 per visit. This is pure mathematics, but it is made to sound ridiculous with an intent to make your economist's mathematics sound overreaching and inappropriate.

When faced with this situation, you can respond in the following way:

> You have promised that you would be governed by the law and the evidence. The only evidence you have heard in regard to future medical expenses is the testimony we presented. Certainly, if there was a dispute, the defense would have brought on evidence to prove our expert wrong. The defendant had no problem bringing on three physicians in regard to what caused the plaintiff's injury. They had no problem bringing on an expert as to how this accident happened. Why didn't they bring on an economist?

> I submit to you that what defense counsel is doing is taking uncontroverted evidence and pure mathematics and trying to claim that it is ridiculous simply because it sounds strange. His

Honor has told you that you must follow the evidence and the law. Why is that? First, evidence comes in under oath, and that's significant. Also, evidence is subject to cross-examination and that's extremely important. In this case, Dr. "G," the life care specialist, and Dr. "A," the economist, have testified as to the dollars I have shown you on this board. These are the uncontroverted figures that you should place in the verdict form.

Defense counsel, through lawyer talk, ridicules the testimony because he has no way to refute it through evidence or expert testimony. This is because in life truth often sounds stranger than fiction. Sometimes the truth is strange. For example, if I were to start with one cent in my bank account, and double the amount of money in my bank account at the end of every week for fifty-two weeks, I would be the richest person in the world. In fact, if I were to start with one penny in the bank, and the next week double it to two cents, and the week after that double it to four cents, and the week after that double it to eight cents, then at the end of fifty-two weeks, I would be worth more than forty trillion dollars. While this seems impossible, it is mathematics, and it is the reason that prices rise so quickly.

I will show you this on the board. At the end of the first week I have two cents, the second week four cents, the third week eight cents, and then 16, 32, 64, $1.28, $2.56, $5.12, $10.24. Round it off to $10.00 at the end of the tenth week. The eleventh week $20, then $40, $80, $160, $320, $640, $1,280, $2,560, $5,120, and $10,240. Round it down to $10,000 at the end of twenty weeks. At the end of thirty weeks it's 10 million dollars; at the end of forty weeks it's 10 billion dollars, and the end of fifty weeks it's 10 trillion dollars, and at the end of fifty-two weeks, it's over 40 trillion dollars.

The Court is going to tell you to govern this case on the law and the evidence, and not on lawyer talk. If the figures that were presented in the evidence were not fair and reasonable, then I submit the defense would have put on evidence, not lawyer talk. Our system of justice is supposed to be a search for the truth. It is not supposed to be an attempt to use lawyer talk to ridicule the truth simply because truth sometimes sounds stranger than fiction.

### When Issues Of Morality That Have No Direct Effect on the Issues in the Case Are Raised

In the nineteenth century, Victor Hugo created a character by the name of Claude Frollo in his book *The Hunchback of Notre Dame*. He is the type of character that was almost universally offensive when that classic book was written, and he remains so even today.

You will try cases in your career where you will be blessed with the opportunity to confront opponents who have a Frollo aura about them in the courtroom. They are quick to be remarkably judgmental about almost every aspect of our society that falls outside their vision of "the norm." They will attack your client for being an unwed mother or for being a heavy drinker or drug user in the past. They will by innuendo and crafty wordsmithing point out that your client is gay or that your client has had an affair or possibly been married far too many times. You should always be aware of why Frollo is so universally disliked, and that is...because people have a great capacity to forgive what they personally might view as a moral transgression. Characters like Frollo have always been offensive in American history and literature because people do not want to believe that they personally ever would be capable of petty, uncompromising, unforgiving prejudice, and bias about most moral issues. When you are confronted with the Frollo character as an opponent in a courtroom, your goal should be to remind the jury that in their hearts, they do have a capacity to forgive. That they in no way want to have a mental image of themselves as being unlikable, unsophisticated, uncompromising fanatics.

Mr. Smith, opposing counsel, believes he has the right to stand before you and judge my client on moral grounds. He believes that the fact that my client is gay has some bearing on whether the defendant ran the red light. Mr. Smith wants to forget that our system of justice is blind to prejudice. The lady who holds the scales of justice wears a blindfold. She wears this blindfold because she does not want to see race, religion, gender, wealth, nationality, or even sexual orientation. She wants to judge everyone by the same standard. She wants a system of justice whereby everyone is treated equally. Mr. Smith apparently does not want you to judge this case on blind justice, because he knows he will lose under the facts and law. Mr. Smith wants you to judge this case on sexual orientation, and this is not how the American justice system is supposed to work. If my client has committed an immoral act, then there are many who believe he will one day be judged by a much higher authority than this jury. Today is not that day of judgment. Today is the day for you, the jury, to determine the facts of this case, and how the law of this country applies to those facts. Today is the day you ask yourself whether or not you are comfortable throwing that first stone.

Ladies and gentlemen: counsel for the defendant has a right to live his life in whatever manner he deems acceptable, as we all do. He has the right to stand before you and by innuendo and suggestion tell you that he does not approve of the way my client lives his life. I am certain that not all of you agree with my client's lifestyle. But what counsel for the defendant does not have the right to do is come before you in this courtroom and hint at the fact, sneak around the fact, that you should punish my client because we don't agree with the way he lives. In Puritan England, severe, mean-spirited community leaders who would dress up in black coats, black pants, black hats, and black shoes, would appoint themselves as a kind of moral police. It was the job of these Puritan community leaders to proclaim that a woman was probably a witch if she had a child out of wedlock. Or that a woman might be unchaste if she wore her skirts too short. My opponent may feel comfortable asking us to play that kind of role here today. But I hope when you go back into the jury room that you call attention to the fact that there is no place for such thinking in an American courtroom. I hope you will remind counsel for the defense of that fact.

## When a Hung Jury Is Better Than a Loss

All of us have experienced or will experience the horror of watching our case burn down in small segments as a trial progresses. As this process takes place and we become adequately certain that total victory is not even a possibility, we need to at least have a plan to salvage what we can for our client. Most of the time in those terminal situations, the best we can hope for is a hung jury. It may be the only chance we have to, at the very least, get our opposition back to the negotiating table after trial.

Juries generally reach an impasse because of the pride one or two jurors have about "their principles." However, "personal principles" are disregarded during jury deliberation when a juror finds himself in a minority of one after a full day of deliberation. That one juror who walked into the jury room to deliberate according to his principles more than likely will find it acceptable to compromise those same principles when two or three more aggressive jurors harangue and harass him about his "unreasonable position." In the end, most jurors will abandon their pride and principles and cave in unless you prepare them to be strong.

If you believe you have a juror who has the makeup to hang onto his convictions in the face of overwhelming odds, you should at least attempt to arm him with as much courage and stamina as you can.

Obviously, the following kind of argument should be used only during rebuttal after you have had every possible opportunity to make a decision about your odds of a long-shot win. In the perfect world, you would be able to hear amens, words of agreement, and maybe even see a few "high fives" between your opponent and a jury majority. This obviously will not occur during a jury trial. The best you will see is strong juror reaction in the form of body and facial reaction.

If what you are hearing, seeing, and feeling during your opponent's closing leads you to believe you and your client are going down the tubes, then you should muster the nerve to argue something similar to the following:

Ladies and gentlemen: I tried a case years ago where a jury could not reach a decision in a trial that had lasted almost a month. That jury was hung, and my client and the other side had another chance to attempt to resolve their differences. The jury was hung because several jurors were unwilling to compromise their personal values, their personal principles about right and wrong. Those jurors did the right thing because they stood behind what they believed to be right.

When you walk back to that jury room, it is not likely that everyone of you will agree or accept what some of the other jurors hold as their opinion in this case. You may, in fact, find yourself completely alone in what you believe is justice in this case. If you find yourself in this position, no matter which side it is, remember this: our democracy has been built and sustained by people with principles and conviction, people who have held onto those principles and convictions in the face of aggressive, loud opposition, humiliation, and even complete rejection by friends and peers.

There is nothing about a civil trial that asks you to abandon your principles. In fact, it is a setting like this where those principles really mean something. It is a setting like this when you can find yourself in a position of having five people against one, with the five people being very demanding and highly charged in attempting to have you agree with something that you do not believe is right. After hours, and possibly even days, of deliberations, things can become extremely heated. It is in this type of setting that a person's true principles and makeup are challenged. Will they back down or will they hold their ground?

If a unanimous verdict is reached in this case, then this case is over; and your decision is final, and both sides will have to live with your verdict. If the jury is unable to reach a unanimous verdict, then both sides will have another day to try their case again or attempt to resolve their differences without a second trial.

### When a Lawyer Appeals to Juror Self-Interests And Prejudices

The insurance industry and corporate America have been extremely effective in the last two decades at convincing potential jurors that jury verdicts directly cause insurance rates to increase and the price of products to rise. For this reason, many jurors have a preconceived notion that if they award your client money, their insurance rates will increase. It is a rare occurrence in personal injury cases that the defense counsel does not attempt to imply this to jurors.

It can be helpful to raise this issue in a motion in limine in order to prevent defense counsel from making these innuendos or direct statements during jury selection and during trial. It is also important to address this issue head-on during voir dire and get a commitment from each juror that they will follow the law and not permit thoughts of self-interest to affect their decision.

Depending upon the circumstances of who is sitting on your jury, and what occurred during trial, you also might want to say something in closing similar to the following:

It has been suggested to you during this trial that if you award Mr. Jones a large sum of money for his injury, somehow it is going to cost you money. That it will cost everyone in this courtroom money out of their pockets. Aside from the fact that it is not true, there are other things you need to consider about that argument. First, it is an argument that invites all of us to be our worst selves. It is an argument that is meant to cause us to focus on negative traits such as greed, insensitivity, and selfishness. The defense is hoping that this will color your ability to be fair to Mr. Jones, that it will color your ability to follow the law, and that it will color your ability to do justice in this case. The defense hopes that you will not be able to put all your potential interests and prejudices aside so that you can follow your obligation as a juror. The defense hopes that it will walk away with a small verdict, a slap on the wrist, and that justice will not prevail.

I am certain that each of you will see what the defense is trying to do, and how wrong it is. I am certain that, as individuals and as a group, you will not allow this process to fall to the point that we trade-off or give up the dignity of our justice system so this corporation can save more money, as opposed to this company investing in and being more concerned with safety and the welfare of others.

Being a juror is one of the most difficult tasks a person can undertake because a juror has to be able to put aside all conceivable thoughts of self-interest and prejudices and apply the law to the evidence, even when they may disagree with the law or the potential impact of the law. But our American system of justice cannot work without each of us agreeing to abide by and follow the law.

One of the greatest feelings a person can have is confidence and pride. It is a great feeling to be able to go up to someone who may disagree with or criticize your decision, and say, "I may not have liked the law or liked the potential consequences, but I did my job. I followed the law, and I would do the same thing again, and would hope the same would be done for me."

### *When the Defendant Admits Liability During Trial*

When defendants admits liability after a trial has begun, they are usually thinking that they can reclaim the moral high ground with the jury and in turn try to minimize damage awards. Unfortunately, lawyers are too often so relieved that they have "won" the liability fight that they become too forgiving and too complacent at the closing argument stage of the trial.

Do not fall into the trap of soft-pedaling or minimizing this event during closing. Rest assured that the defense has probably not admitted liability out of their sense of fair play and justice, and it is a critical mistake to telegraph "forgiveness" to the jury in your closing argument.

When this trial first began, this corporation and its lawyers stood up in front of you and denied the fact that the company was clearly responsible for the chain of events that led to the death of

Mr. Higby. You might remember that the lawyers for that corporation stood up here in front of you with a straight face and told you that someone else is responsible. They already had all the facts we have presented in the course of this trial. They had all the testimony by way of depositions. They already knew what the witnesses would say. What the experts would say. They had already read all the documents. They had seen all the evidence that we had to present in this trial. But you know what? They made us spend our money and your time to bring in all those witnesses to say what they knew all along. That is, that this company created the chain of events that led to Mr. Higby's death. So, now what is it that they want you to believe? Well, after a week-long trial, they want you to believe that their act of admitting what they have done is somehow noble and honorable. And they are hoping that by telling you that they are noble and honorable in doing what they should have done before we started this trial, they will persuade you to forgive them and award less damages to Mr. Higby's widow. That is the only reason that they have admitted their fault three years after Mr. Higby's death.

The truth is, ladies and gentlemen, this corporation has been gambling for the last three years. And the chips they have been using are made up of all the anguish they have put Mr. Higby's family through. All of the fear, all of the uncertainty they have placed on the shoulders of the Higby family for three long years. Depositions, interrogatories, detailed discovery requests, the personal humiliation of this whole process. Those are the chips this corporation has used to gamble. Their gamble was that they could beat this family down and make this lawsuit go away. Their gamble was that they could now stand before you and appear noble and honorable and ask you to go easy on them with your money damage award. I hope this corporation lost that very expensive gamble, ladies and gentlemen. And I hope you will tell them that with your verdict.

### *When the Defense Lawyer Tries to Laugh You out of Court*

There are a handful of defense lawyers who have mastered the technique of minimizing the seriousness and importance of the trial process, regardless of how severe the injuries may be, and regardless of how reprehensible the conduct of their client may be. These lawyers usually take on a folksy demeanor and try to ingratiate themselves with the jury by joking with the venire and telling homespun little stories about their spouse, their children, their grandparents, their dog, and so on. These lawyers recognize that most jurors want to be in a setting where the pressure is off in regard to the seriousness of the matters they must decide.

Most of the time, the plaintiff's lawyer has absolutely no benefit in lessening the juror's sense of responsibility in a jury trial. Therefore, if the defense lawyer has a jury laughing, then the plaintiff's lawyer is probably losing.

It is important to take some affirmative deliberate steps to put an end to the relaxed carnival atmosphere that the defense lawyer is hoping will be carried back into the jury room:

Ladies and gentlemen: In the course of this trial, I've caught myself chuckling occasionally because of a few things that have occurred, and maybe even laughing about a story or comment or two that counsel for the defense has made in the last few days.

And when I caught myself laughing, I would always lean over and mention to my client that my laugher and your laughter is okay because, as I told her, when you go back in that jury room you will clearly understand, in fact, everyone in this courtroom understands, that even though we have been able to laugh and relax a few times in the course of this trial; everyone in this courtroom absolutely understands how very serious this case is.

I explained to her that jurors don't decide a case according to who makes them laugh the most or who can tell the most folksy stories. If that were the case, this corporation would always hire comedians and storytellers.

I felt comfortable telling Mrs. Jones that simply because there have been a few laughs, a few stories that have been knocked around this courtroom the last few days, that does not mean that you, as jurors, would not go back into the jury room, roll up your sleeves, and do the hard work, and recognize how serious your job really is. I know you might have laughed at the jokes told by the lawyer who represents this corporation, but I am certain you would never see anything funny or humorous about the conduct that this corporation has engaged in for the past decade. You know, if I were calling the shots for a corporation like this, I suppose I would want the focus of what we are really here about to turn toward stories and comments that put a softer, happier edge onto what we have heard in this courtroom this week.

### Combating the Defense's Use of Innuendo and Gossip

Many times in trial defense counsel will attempt to poison jurors toward your client with subtle suggestions and statements that approach almost a gossip or innuendo quality. Defense counsel may not blatantly make a statement about your client because to do so would make him appear too judgmental or too harsh. And, in fact, he may not make the statement because he realizes that it simply is not true even though it may be plausible or believable. These types of "gossipy" innuendo-like suggestions usually center around facts that might lead jurors to believe that your client is a bad mother, or your client was unfaithful to his spouse, or that your client beat her children.

98

It is an attempt by the defense to throw a little bad gossip against the wall and hope some of it registers and influences at least a few of the jurors. Do not treat it as if it never happened:

> Ladies and gentlemen: I am not sure about this, but you know a couple of times in this trial I thought I heard counsel for the defense ask questions and make statements that tried to suggest that maybe my client was a bad mother. If I didn't know better, it almost sounded like Mr. Wipple, counsel for the defense, was trying to create issues in this trial that fell to the level of pure garden-variety gossip that was not based on anything we have heard or seen in this trial. That's because what he tried to suggest to you by innuendo simply is not true, and he knows it. He wouldn't have come out and made the statement that my client is a bad mother because he knows that that just is not true. Instead, what he wanted to do was simply plant that seed in your mind and hope a few of you would buy into his gossip mentality. His mother might not have taught him what Sheila has no doubt taught her children: that is, that gossip is usually the most pathetic form of dishonesty.

### Answering the Defendant's Attempt to Lowball Damages

The reason the defense lawyer attempts to make a lowball damage argument in every single jury trial is that they understand that very often this kind of argument is successful. Do not assume that jurors will easily recognize this tactic on their own:

> The first car I ever owned I drove for five years. I took perfect care of that car. I washed it and waxed it almost every week. Always changed the oil. The outside was perfect, its engine was perfect, the interior was like new. But when I went to sell that car everyone who said they wanted to buy it told me that they wouldn't pay what I was asking. They always wanted to offer

about half of the selling price. I learned that in the car business, they call that a lowball offer. In the car business, they know that statistically a large number of people will accept a lowball offer no matter how unfair it is, no matter how inappropriate the offer is. In the end, I sold that well-kept car for exactly what I was asking. I sold it for what it was really worth. I didn't agree to an unfair compromise because I knew I had honestly and fairly put a value on that car. Counsel for the defense sounded an awful lot like those people in the car business during his closing statement. The numbers he suggested to you sounded just as unfair and inappropriate as if they were being spoken between two people on a car lot haggling, trying to lowball each other over the price of a car.

Ladies and gentlemen: The numbers I have put up on the board don't reflect any attempt on my part to haggle or car trade with this corporation. That is simply inappropriate in a setting as serious as this. The numbers up here on this board are real; they are fair; they appropriately reflect the loss, the suffering, and the anguish this family has suffered. For this corporation to fall to the level of paying pennies on the dollar like we might see on a used car lot demeans the value and importance of this family's lives.

## Chapter 6
## DAMAGE ARGUMENTS AND STARTING POINTS

There are truly some great technical trial lawyers practicing law today. They have a sound command of the textbook techniques for presenting their cases. Some are tremendous tacticians. Others are gifted cross-examiners who have the ability to progress toward the closing argument ahead of their opponent because they have completely dismantled their opponent's case. Still others may not have sound foundations in the art of trying a case, but their charisma, charm, and good common sense put them in a place where they are usually winning their case by the time closing arguments are to be delivered. There is one thing that is common to all of those lawyers. In fact, there is a universal trait that applies to all types of trial lawyers. That truth is this: if they do not know how to ask for money for their client during closing statement, then no matter how far ahead they are prior to closing statement; they will have done a disservice to their client.

Professional salespeople understand that the step of asking for money in the process of finalizing a sale is so important that they specially train people called "closers" for that purpose. One salesman dedicates his efforts to put all of the parts of the sale together in a way that is better than his competition, and then the "closer" is brought in to ask for the money.

Most trial lawyers do not have the luxury of having a specially trained money closer to show up at trial and help out during the time that we have the responsibility to argue damages. It is simply part of our job to be effective money closers relying solely on our own ability.

In "Section A" below, we provide complete sample damage arguments. In the following "Section B," we provide sample damage starting points to be utilized as part of a damage argument.

## A. Sample Damage Arguments

### Wrongful Death Generally

If a medical doctor was killed because of the fault of another, it does not take a brilliant trial attorney to put on an economist to testify to the loss of past and future income. In most states, however, the survivors are also entitled to compensation for mental pain and suffering. The following argument, and variations of the same, has been used by the authors in all different types of wrongful death cases:

> Many of us have suffered the loss of a loved one during our life but have never recovered money for that loss. Why should Mr. Smith recover money? The answer is simple: the law of Florida recognizes that the loss of a loved one is a traumatic and tragic experience. We want to do everything we can to stop these experiences from happening unnaturally. We want others to act responsibly and with due care. In this case, the law provides only one type of remedy to help assure that one acts reasonably and with due care, and it is in the form of monetary damages. There is no criminal trial that will occur and no crime that can be charged as the result of Mrs. Smith's dying. We no longer have a society where we say, "You killed my wife as a result of negligence, and therefore, one of your family must die." We do not have a society where the punishment is "an eye for an eye and a tooth for a tooth." The only remedy for Mr. Smith is the compensation you award today. That is the law.

The question you are likely asking is: "How do you possibly put a figure on the loss of someone we love?" There unfortunately is no exact measurement or formula. One thing we know is that many times we do place some monetary value on the loss of a loved one. Think about the times an individual is lost at sea in a boat or a plane. We don't hesitate to send helicopters, the Coast Guard, boats, divers, and hundreds of men and women to search for the person. We never stop to ask the person's race, or gender, or age, or social status. Certainly no one would criticize an Air Force pilot for bailing out of a failing multimillion-dollar aircraft to save his or her own life.

While society does place monetary value on life every day, that is not the standard of compensation in the state of Florida. In Florida, you must determine how much Mr. Smith has suffered and will suffer over the loss of his wife. How do you put a figure on this? One way is to think about the example of a baby crib that may have been in a family 100 years and passed down from generation to generation. One day I decide to send the crib to my daughter who lives in South Florida and is having a baby. On the way down, the crib gets misplaced. When I call the trucking company about the crib, they say it was accidentally lost; but that they can get a new crib for $200, and they offer me $200. I try to explain to them that the crib has a lot of sentimental value to me, and that it is worth much more than $200. The trucking company refuses to pay more than the $200 because it says it cannot place a figure on my sentimental value.

The question is how do we determine what the crib is really worth to me? One way to determine what it is worth to me is to determine what I am willing to give up for it. For example, if I had put an ad in the paper offering $10,000 to anyone who finds the crib, then you know it is worth that amount to me, and that is what my mental loss is. The same is true here. The question is what would Mr. Smith be willing to pay or give up to have his wife back. It is easy to say $10,000,000 because he doesn't have it. But what if he gave up something worth $10,000,000? If Mr. Smith were involved in a motor vehicle accident and were unable to walk and were in a wheelchair for life, there would be little difficulty awarding him $10,000,000 for this loss. Thus, Mr. Smith does have something worth $10,000,000, the use of his legs. I submit to you that if Mr. Smith had the choice of living in a wheelchair for the rest of his life and still having his wife, he would certainly give up his legs to have his wife back. This is a way to place value on Mr. Smith's loss.

You may be asking yourself the question, what good is the money going to do? We all know that the money can't bring a loved one back, but that is not the issue here. The issue is how much pain the unnatural death has caused to Mr. Smith and how much Mr. Smith will continue to suffer. Also, the money does help to tell Mr. Smith that you, the jury, recognize what has been done is wrong and should not have happened, that you recognize that Mr. Smith is suffering and will continue to suffer. The money also gives Mr. Smith a chance to do something in honor of his wife; for example, start a scholarship in her name, or construct a building in her name, or do some of the things that she always wanted for her family.

We live in a strange society. Athletes and actors are paid tens of millions of dollars a year. Yet, today we are here trying to evaluate Mr. Smith's loss of his wife. Mrs. Smith was not famous and was not a star. Very few people even knew who she was. She was one of the many faces in the crowd. But to Mr. Smith she was the most important person in the world. She was funny, intelligent, caring, and his best friend. Few people knew her, but to Mr. Smith she was the biggest hero and most famous person in the world.

*The Wrongful Death of a Problem Child*

You will likely be faced with a situation whereby a parent has lost a wayward child—the "black sheep" of the family. The issue is how to argue these types of damages so that the jurors can understand your client's loss even in light of the fact that the deceased child does not generate much sympathy from the jury. The following argument is not the kind of argument that could be used in most settings, but in the particular setting where it was argued by the authors, it was effective in overcoming an extremely destructive taint that had been placed on a deceased child. The argument is also an example of a willingness to step outside the box...to take a few chances and argue like the creative, entertaining, artistic storyteller that most trial lawyers have the ability to be.

What is it about the loss of a child that causes so much pain to the parent? Most parents have more than one child or can have other children. So why is there so much pain over the loss of one child? It could be that each child provides something very special in an individual way. No two children are alike. One may be a smart child, one may be athletic, one may be kind, and one may be mischievous.

I realize and accept that John Smith was not the ideal son and that he was not kind to his mother. I appreciate what defense counsel stated in regard to John not being a valuable member of society. He was constantly in trouble. He had drug problems, he had been in prison, and he had trouble keeping a job. But that is not the measure of damages under Florida law. The law is to evaluate the loss that Mrs. Smith now feels and will continue to feel over John's premature death. The measure of damages is not what this community feels by John's death, but what Mrs. Smith, John's mother, feels by the loss of her son.

John caused his mother many sleepless nights, but she never stopped loving him, and she cared for him deeply. She only wanted the best for her son. I don't know what it is that causes a mother and child to bond. It must be something deeply biological. It must be the fact that she carried him for nine months and he grew within her. There is no love like the love of a mother for her child. There is no bond stronger than that of a mother and child, no matter how awful the act of the child may have been. No matter how disturbing or reprehensible the conduct of the child becomes, a mother and a child are joined at the heart.

I would like to tell you an old Chinese fable that is very appropriate to this case. This fable tells of a mother and her son who lived alone on one side of the forest. The son was in his late teens and had very little going for him. He was not a very impressive character by anybody's standards. The son was madly in love with a beautiful young Chinese girl who lived on the other side of the forest. Almost daily, the young boy would go to the home of the beautiful young maiden and express his love for her. The problem was that the maiden had no feelings whatsoever for the young man and attempted everything to get rid of him. The young girl realized that this unattractive suitor loved his mother dearly and that his mother had raised him from the time he was an infant. The maiden came up with a plan that she was certain would get rid of her troublesome suitor. The young Chinese girl told the boy that she would marry him, but only on one condition, and that was for him to bring to her the heart of his mother. Of course, the young man said he could not kill his mother that he loved so dearly. But the maiden persisted and told him that she never wanted to see him again unless he would bring to her his mother's heart. Days passed into weeks and the young man's love became overwhelming. Finally, one evening, in the early hours of the morning, the young Chinese boy took a knife and went into his mother's bedroom. He drove the knife into her chest and cut out her heart. The young Chinese boy picked up the heart in his hands and started running through the woods to take his mother's heart to the girl he wanted to marry. In his excitement, he was running and did not notice the root of a tree that crossed his path. The young man tripped over the root and fell to the ground and the heart rolled out of his hands. From the heart came these words: "Have you hurt yourself, my son? Are you all right?"

No one can understand the unshakeable love that a mother has for her son. The world might find the son repulsive, but to the mother, he is everything. It is what she cherishes and what she lives for. It is what brings her joy and pain, but most important, what makes her know she is alive. It is not for others to judge what is best for the mother; it is for the mother to decide. Today you are not to decide society's loss, or your loss, or Defense counsel's loss, or my loss. You are to decide Ms. Smith's loss, and the pain and emptiness she now feels. For many years, society has been telling Ms. Smith that her son was worthless. To Ms. Smith this meant that she was worthless, because she is the one who bore and raised her son. Please do not let your jury verdict tell Ms. Smith that her son was worthless.

*Pain and Suffering Damages*

Asking for a pain and suffering damage award is very difficult, because there is no guideline the court will provide the jury. There is no jury instruction and no defined measure. Also, damage awards for pain and suffering are controversial, and have been the subject of much insurance propaganda, such as the McDonald's coffee cup case. Many jurors are not inclined to award pain and suffering damages, much less large awards. Moreover, some jurors think that $100,000 is a huge sum for pain and suffering over the loss of a limb, while others think millions are more appropriate. Pain and suffering damages are not like medical expenses or wage loss, which are both subject to mathematical calculations. For this reason, the trial lawyer needs to be able to provide guidance to the jury through very appropriate and clear analogies.

The following is a sample argument regarding valuing pain and suffering:

> We next get to the final form of damages, and that is pain and suffering, disability, disfigurement, mental anguish, and loss of capacity for the enjoyment of life experienced in the past and in the future. There is no measurement for these damages. There's no way to sit here and put a dollar figure on Mike White's condition. The jury instruction says to use your common sense and experience.

> Trial lawyers throughout history have struggled with the idea of how to convey their client's suffering. They stay up for nights attempting to think of analogies that will assist the jurors in placing a monetary figure on something that neither is sold in stores nor can be purchased.

> But what if it could be purchased? What if someone was in the business of paying people to experience Mike's lifestyle? What would someone have to pay an individual to live like Mike White? A newspaper ad might read something like the following:

> Wanted: A 34-year-old individual who is willing to live permanently in a wheelchair; who will have no ability to move his legs; who will have constant leg spasms throughout the day

that are so violent and painful that his legs will stiffen up. The job applicant will be in constant pain, and there is no cure for the pain, no medication, and no drugs. Every four hours he is going to have to catheterize himself to empty his bladder. Every two to three days, he is going to have to empty his own bowels. As he ages, the pain is going to get more intense because the pain is caused by sitting, yet all he can do is sit. As the job applicant gets older, it's going to be more difficult for him to transfer himself from the chair to the toilet, from the toilet to the shower, from the shower to the bed; and as he ages, the job applicant is going to need assistance with his daily living care, people to help him transfer, and people to help clean him. The job applicant will have few friends, no girlfriend, no sexual companionship, and no children. The only peace he will get is when he sleeps and dreams, yet he will only sleep two to three hours at a time because the pain will wake him up.

This job is obviously not appealing, and yet there is one more major catch to the job. That is, once you accept the job, you can never quit it, never. Once you accept the offer, it's for life. Mike White didn't voluntarily accept this job, and no one would. For four years he's had it, and for thirty-five years in the future he will have it.

The only peace and enjoyment Mike gets in life is when he sleeps approximately four hours a day. When sleeping, he says he dreams he is walking, working, and fishing. He is going out to dinner and to movies with his wife, and he is attending his son's school and athletic functions. He is then suddenly awakened by his pain and realizes that he has been awakened from a beautiful dream and remembers that his real life is a nightmare.

How much would we have to pay someone an hour to have voluntarily accepted this job? No one but no one would accept it.

But what if it was just $100 an hour? You take $100 an hour times 20 hours a day times 365 days, and it's $25 million in the future.

*Loss of Enjoyment of Life*

Not long ago the authors tried a case involving a nineteen-year-old girl who suffered a severe brain injury. The difficulty with the case was that the brain injury was so severe that the girl did not experience physical pain or mental pain. The injury had left her with a childlike persona that made her appear extremely happy and content with her new life. The most important part of the closing was selling the concept of enjoyment of life. The following argument resulted in a twenty-two million-dollar jury verdict:

> How can a price possibly be placed on enjoyment of life? To some people enjoyment of life can be the relationship they share with their spouse, or their children, or with friends, or with the church, or playing sports, or experiencing the outdoors, or accomplishments in their personal life. For each individual, enjoyment of life means something different, and depending upon which stage of life a person is at, enjoyment of life changes. Probably the best way to describe enjoyment of life is to say it is someone's freedom of choice. It is freedom to decide where a person wants to live, whom a person wants to share time with, what a person wishes to do, and a person's ability to change his or her mind at any time during life to do something different.

> For example, Mary Campbell will never experience the unforgettable sensation of falling in love, getting married, and having children. She will not have the choice of experiencing the joy that comes with watching a child crawl for the first time, walk for the first time, speak for the first time, say the amazing things that children can say, watch them attend their first days of school

and watch them come home and want to explain in detail everything that occurred to them. Mary will never have the sensation of watching her child mature into adulthood and become an independent person. She will never watch her children walk down an aisle to get married. She will never have the choice of being able to attend the birth of her grandchildren. Mary has approximately fifty-nine years of life to live. During that time, she will either be at home with her parents or in a facility. During the time she is in a facility, there is no way to know who will be working with her, what their motivations might be, what their background might be, or whether their intentions are good or bad. Mary has no way to defend herself from the evils in life and evil people. She is susceptible to the bad and has no way to take action to help make sure she is safe. Mary can only be as happy and safe as the persons who are caring for her allow her to be. It is as if she is buried in the sand up to her head. She is totally vulnerable to everyone and everything around her because she has no way to protect herself.

The childlike smile that we have seen on Mary's face is not a smile that should lead us to believe that Mary would choose this life for herself if she had a choice. It is a smile that masks the tragedy of what has occurred in her life.

*Damages for Physical Disfigurement*

When faced with a plaintiff who suffers from noticeable physical disfigurements, you can attempt an argument such as the following:

Pick up any magazine at any store in America, and you will note that almost every other advertisement is devoted to telling us how we can improve our appearance. Advertisements will tell us how we can improve the appearance of our skin. How we can change and improve the color and texture of our hair. Madison

111

Avenue is forever telling the American Public that beauty, appearance, and physical looks really do matter in our society. I've heard estimates that Americans collectively spend more than 150 billion dollars a year buying products designed to improve their appearance, products that are designed to make them more pleasing to look at. In our American culture, like it or not, appearance really matters. The people who have studied physical appearance in our culture tell us that, unfortunately, how we look can even impact our education and our job careers.

America's obsession with physical perfection even begins with our children, when manufacturers of Barbie dolls create characteristics that are almost humanly impossible to achieve. But it sends a message to our children that perfection in physical appearance really matters.

In today's time when you pick up a magazine and look at an advertisement picturing America's supermodels, believe it or not, even those physically perfect people are not perfect enough. Thus, the editors of the magazines have the models airbrushed to the point that every single blemish has been removed.

Well, there will be no airbrushing available to remove the scars that are now permanently a part of Mrs. Jones' physical appearance. Not a single one of all of those cosmetic products available for women is going to do a bit of good to cover up those scars. When Mrs. Jones walks into a room full of strangers, there is no doubt in her mind that in an instant everyone in that room will have judged her according to that standard of physical perfection that our culture admires whether we want to admit it or not.

And you know what? Even as hard as Mrs. Jones has tried, even she judges herself by those standards. Standards she has lived with for thirty years of her life before this accident. And just as you heard her say on the stand, even when other people may not show that they are aware of those scars, even when out of politeness or pity, other people act like they are unaware of those scars, even then, Mrs. Jones still knows they are there. Just as they will be for the forty-five years left in her life.

But Mrs. Jones' pain from the scarring doesn't end her physical disfigurement. Everyday when Mrs. Jones wakes up and looks in the mirror or sees her reflection in glass, she doesn't only see her horrendous scars, she sees the defendant's truck running the red light and hitting her car. She sees her gas tank exploding and her struggle to undo her seatbelt. She feels the heat burning her skin. She hears her own screams of pain and agony. She hears the shrill of the bystanders helpless to approach her vehicle. She sees herself in the hospital for 6 months and crying hysterically while being placed in the whirlpool to remove the dead skin. Every day when Mrs. Jones sees her own image, she sees a lot more than the disfigurement that all of us see.

*Arguing Damages in Minor Injury Cases*

It is very difficult to get juries to award damages in minor injury cases. Juries believe these types of injuries are common and often exaggerated, and have no significant impact on the victim. The following is a suggested argument in a case involving minor injuries:

This case certainly has not been the type of trial we see on TV with all of that Hollywood-generated excitement and emotion that keep us at the edge of our seat. It is not a dramatic murder case or even a multimillion-dollar injury case. In fact, I am certain that a few of you have wondered why a jury needs to waste its time deciding a case involving a minor neck and back injury.

However, if we as society do not believe that this type of case should proceed before a jury, then we are saying that when someone suffers minor injuries because of the fault of another, he is not entitled to compensation. If we as society believe these cases have very little monetary value, then we are saying that when someone suffers minor injuries because of the fault of another, the value of the case is so low that it is not economically feasible for the injured person to hire a lawyer or go to court. What we would then be saying is that someone who receives minor injuries must simply bear the burden of his own injury, even if the injury was caused by another person.

This is not how our system of justice works. Our system of justice is based on the theory that there should be a right for every wrong. That we should decide our disputes by relying on a jury system rather than choosing to take the law into our own hands.

Mrs. Smith is a homemaker. Twenty-four hours a day she is at the call of her children. She cooks for them, shops for them, cleans for them, drives them to numerous places they have to go. She is responsible for making sure the house is in proper repair, and that things are fixed when they break. She is responsible for making sure that all bills are paid, and when her family is unable to afford to pay the bills, she has to make sure she gets a proper extension so that they do not get evicted from their home, and the electricity and water are kept on.

When Mrs. Smith was growing up, she envisioned a much different life for herself. As a young girl, she dreamed about a life that she never imagined would be as challenging, as tedious, as trying as the life that most of the time comes with being a mother and wife in the twenty-first century. She never dreamed that so many lives would be counting on her to be the best homemaker she could be. But this was not reality.

Mrs. Smith accepted the position she was in before this accident, even though it was not the life she dreamed of as a child, and she always did her job very well. She has been described by everyone as a wonderful wife, mother, and friend.

Mrs. Smith very early on discovered that to be the best she could be for her family, she needed at least a minimal amount of life for herself. She took up bowling two nights a week, and she thoroughly enjoyed it. It was her free time. Her time to get away. Her time to relax and forget about her problems. The accident Mrs. Smith was involved in was minor, and the injury is minor, but unfortunately it has changed Mrs. Smith's life. She can still do everything for her children and her husband, and she can keep up the house, but she no longer has the ability to carve out that little part of life that has always been uniquely hers. That small but important slice of life that allows her to breathe, recharge her batteries, and then jump back in and be the daily anchor for her family. This injury may not have significantly changed another person's life, but to Mrs. Smith her loss is very real. The Court will instruct you that you must evaluate how this injury has impacted Mrs. Smith, not how it would have impacted another person.

*TV Guide* once reported that most Americans would not accept $1 million if they had to give up something as simple as watching television and movies for the rest of their lives. People would not give up television, even for $1 million, because they understood the importance of having a means to escape from our everyday stresses and responsibilities. They felt like the lost of that relaxation would affect the quality of their lives.

I am not suggesting that Mrs. Smith's loss is worth $1 million, but I do suggest that the relaxation bowling provided Mrs. Smith is just as real as the relaxation that television provides to most people. You will hear an instruction from the judge about quality-of-life damages. Please do not minimize the importance of those quality of life damages as they relate to Mrs. Smith's life.

## B. Sample Starting Points

*Wrongful Death Generally*

- We live in a very strange society. If Michael Jordan had been involved in an accident that was not his fault and the defendant had caused him to break a bone, which would have prevented Michael from playing professional basketball for a year, there would be no problem awarding him $20,000,000. Yet today we are here trying to evaluate Mr. Smith's loss of his wife. Mrs. Smith was not famous and was not a star. Very few people even knew who she was. She was one of the many faces in the crowd. But to Mr. Smith, she was the most important person in the world. She was funny, intelligent, caring, and his best friend. Few people knew her, but to Mr. Smith, she was the biggest hero and most famous person in the world.

- Today, you must place a value on human life. How can we even attempt to come up with a value? One thing we know is that virtually every day we do place some form of value on life. Think about the times an individual is lost at sea in a boat or a plane. We don't hesitate to send helicopters, the Coast Guard, boats, divers, and hundreds of men and women to search for the person. Certainly no one would criticize an Air Force pilot for bailing out of a failing 40 million-dollar aircraft to save his or her own life. When considering spending money to save a stranded person in a perilous situation, we never stop to ask the person's race, or gender, or age, or social status. We all recognize the value of life.

- We have all heard the saying that time heals all wounds, but we must remember that the wounds leave lasting scars.

- From early childhood men are taught that they should protect their families. They are to be in control, to be strong and never scared, and be able to fix things. Showing emotion is labeled weak or pitiful. Men are expected to be strong under adverse circumstances. Men are taught that painful feelings should be repressed. Repressed grief, however, lasts much longer than acknowledged grief and can lead to complications. For many men, the longer their grief remains repressed, the more reluctant they are to allow it to surface.

- It is difficult for a person to come to grips with the fact that he or she did not have the opportunity to say, "I love you," "I am sorry," "Thank you," and "Goodbye."

- Last year, I read where a painting, admittedly a Van Gogh, sold for $63 million at an auction house in New York. Sixty-three million dollars. Well, now, if somebody were hauling that painting across town, and another person or company negligently ran into them and destroyed the painting, then clearly the owner of the painting should be entitled to $63 million in damages, because that is the worth of the painting. That is what he paid for it. That is what he lost. But today we are talking about a loss much greater than an oil painting. We are talking about the greatest work of art, the greatest creation, ever. We are talking about life. What Mr. Smith lost on February 4, 2004, was much more valuable than a painting.

- If the law had permitted you to speak to Mrs. Jones during the portion of this trial when she was telling you about the loss she feels over the death of her husband, I am certain that every person on this jury would have wanted to speak words of comfort, compassion, and hope to her. The law does not permit you to do this. Instead, the law says that you must speak to Mrs. Jones through your verdict. It is through that piece of paper that you tell Mrs. Jones that you believe her, that her husband's life did have value, and that the impact of the loss of her husband has turned her life upside-down.

- During his closing argument, defense counsel started off by telling you that he did not want to talk about money damages because he said you should not even get to that question. He then went on for twenty-minutes talking about damages, and telling you that the $3,000,000 we have asked you to award is absurd and insulting. He said that for the plaintiff, this case is all about money. It is not about justice. The defendant still doesn't get it. This case is not about money. This case is about the fact that they killed Mr. Jones as a result of their negligence, and they did not acknowledge it three years ago and do not acknowledge it today. To the defendant, they did nothing wrong and Mrs. Jones is simply trying to get money. The only remedy in Florida for this type of situation is for you, the jury, to determine what Mrs. Jones lost when her husband was killed. This is admittedly difficult to do. There is no mathematical calculation that can be applied. However, if the defense wants to talk about it all being about money, then let's talk about money. If the defense put $3 million in cash on this table right now in front of Mrs. Jones and told her that she could take the money and leave the courtroom, or she could return the money, sit in this courtroom, and Mr. Jones would walk in here and take her home; then you can be certain that the $3 million would be on the defendant's table. There is no way Mrs. Jones would take the $3 million if she instead could have her husband walk into this courtroom right now and take her home. This is how you know that a $3 million award is not only reasonable, but is in fact not enough to compensate Mrs. Jones.

*Death of a Child*

- When you lose a parent, it is like losing your past. When you lose a spouse, it is like losing the present. When you lose a child, it is like losing your future.

- From the time that a child first gets out of the crib and begins his first steps across the floor until the time of adulthood, it is the hands of the parents that help the child to his feet and that guide and support the child. But as life goes on, and the aging process continues, it is the steps of the parents that begin to falter. It is at this time that the hands of the child reach out to guide and support the parents.

- What is this loss that you, the jury, are being called upon to measure? It is difficult for me to express. Others, however, have said things much better than I ever will be able to, and for this reason, I would now like to share with you an example of prose entitled "What Is a Boy?":

  > Between the innocence of babyhood and the dignity of manhood, we find the delightful creature called a boy. Boys come in assorted sizes, but all boys have the same creed: to enjoy every second of every minute, every hour of every day, and to protest with noise, which is their only weapon.

  > When the last minute is finished, and mom and dad pack them off to bed at night, boys are found everywhere. On top of, underneath, inside of, climbing, emerging from, running around or jumping to.

  > Little boys: mothers love them, older sisters tolerate them, and heaven protects them. A boy is a magical creature. You can lock him out of your workshop, but you can't lock him out of your heart.

  > You can get him out of your study, but you can't get him out of your mind. You might as well give up. He's your captor, your jailer, your boss. A pint-sized cat chasing a bundle of noise. But when you come home at night with only the shattered pieces of your hopes and dreams after a long day's

work, that little boy can mend all of those problems just like new, with two magic words: "Hi, dad," "Hi, mom."

- Parents have extremely strong feelings for their children. They want to care for their children, to solace them, to help them be content and happy. Parents feel good when their children feel good. It can be almost intolerable for parents to see their children in pain and be unable to help. Parents invest themselves in their children. They give their children energy and attention and caring. They see their children carrying on their love and nurturance into the future. If the children do well, parents feel they are doing well too. Parents can feel blessed in their children. Parents see their children going on into the future and continuing their own lives, and thus, parents feel that what they do for their children, they do for themselves. When a child is killed, the parents' hopes and dreams for that child are totally lost, and so are many of the hopes and dreams the parents had for themselves.

- As Abraham Lincoln said upon the death of his son: "If the pain I now feel were somehow divided equally among all the persons in the world so that each person experienced only the slightest fraction of the pain I presently feel, there still could not be one smiling face in the entire world."

- When someone casually asks Mrs. Jones, "How many children do you have?" how is Mrs. Jones supposed to respond? What is the correct answer?

- Mr. and Mrs. Jones have lost every opportunity and emotion we get the pleasure of sharing with our children. They have lost the ability to have their children sit on their lap, hug and kiss them, and say they love them. They have lost the opportunity to drive their children to school, meet their friends and teachers, attend their school plays, review their report cards, teach them how to play sports, respect others, and prepare for adulthood. They have lost the opportunity to attend graduations and bless marriages. They have lost the opportunity to share the good times and bad times with their children, and they have lost the opportunity to have grandchildren and to start the process all over again.

- There is not a person breathing in this courtroom who would fail to reach for their own child, who would fail to grab for their own son or daughter before they reached for their wallet or pocketbook if they were threatened with even a minor risk of danger. If Mr. and Mrs. Jones had simply had the opportunity to reach for—to save the life of their child, they would have traded every dollar talked about in this trial just for that chance.

*Death of a Spouse*

- Today you must place a value on the suffering Mr. Jones has experienced and will continue to experience as a result of the loss of his wife, a woman he had been married to for more than fifteen years. How do you possibly even start to determine an amount of money to compensate for the loss of a spouse? Marriage is such an amazing thing. As a married couple, we hardly notice that our partner, in almost imperceptible increments, begins to take on an appearance different from the image we first saw when we exchanged wedding vows. As we grow old together, we seldom really notice the new wrinkles that tend to appear on our faces as the years pass. The truth is that all the superficial elements of our relationship as husband and wife become secondary to the fact that in a good marriage a husband and a wife are best friends. We are best friends who remember and record everything about each other. Our wives can tell us every detail about our wedding day, while husbands might remember and record the excitement that occurred with the birth of a first child. Our wives remember that long list of the funniest things we ever said or did, while the husband remembers every detail about a family vacation. We record our lives together as we grow old together. We are to each other the equivalent of a living, breathing camera that records and recalls the most important moments in our lives together. We record for each other as husband and wife all of those memories both good and bad that make up who we are. And we know that there is not another person walking this earth who records and values those memories more than our wife, more than our husband. In a marriage, we both become one. That is one reason a husband feels like he has lost part of his own life when he has lost the companionship of his wife.

• Mr. Jones not only lost his wife of twenty-five years, and the mother of his three children, and his best friend, but he lost the person who stood by him during bad times, sad times, difficult times, and trying times. He lost the person who believed in him when others did not. He lost the person who would be there for him in the future when age slows his mind and health, and when company is rare. He lost the person whom he went to bed with and woke up with each and every day with three simple words: "I love you."

*Pain and Suffering: General Arguments*

• The question I would like you to ask yourself is whether you believe that Mr. Jones would pay $20,000 a year not to suffer from his injuries if he had that amount of money. If you believe he would, then that is the value of his suffering and the amount of pain and suffering damages you should award. If you believe that he would pay more, then his suffering is more.

• I would like you to assume that you, the jury, had the power to bring Mr. Jones before you and make him an offer. The offer is that you will totally erase his scarring, physical pain, mental pain, disability, and all thoughts of the incident, or you will give him

122

$200,000. If you believe that Mr. Jones would tell you to keep the $200,000, but give him his health back, then even $200,000 is not adequate to compensate him for his injuries.

- Almost everyone has had the experience of being seriously ill and laid up in bed. During the time of illness, people begin to realize how precious good health is and how they would be frightened if their normal health did not return and they could not continue with their daily activities of life. People begin to realize what it would be like not to be able to get out of bed easily, or bathe, or groom themselves, or eat food, or get out of the house and continue with life in a normal manner. Finally, one day we wake up and the illness is gone and normal health has returned, and we are temporarily rejuvenated and appreciate life. Unfortunately, for Mr. Jones, he will never wake up with the illness gone and have that sense of rejuvenation that his health is back. Every day he wakes up realizing that his health is gone forever.

- Jason is the person everyone stares at when he is walking down the street, in the mall, grocery store, theater, restaurant. He is the person children point at and state loudly: "Mom/Dad, look at that person. What happened?" He is the person who is noticeably different from everyone else and who has no ability to change this. And he will be reminded of this every day he looks in the mirror and goes out in public. That is the kind of mental pain and suffering the law says should be compensated.

- The Constitution of the United States does not allow the states to inflict pain on even the worst criminals. The law forbids cruel and unusual punishment. We are permitted to take someone's life, but it must be done without pain.

- It is difficult to listen to someone's story about the pain they have known or the suffering they have experienced. It is difficult because it scares us. It makes us feel vulnerable. It makes us dwell on something that makes us uncomfortable. Everyone in this courtroom has a survival mechanism that, thank goodness, protects us from giving too much thought to how harsh life can be when terrible things happen. But today, back in that jury room, you won't have that luxury. You will have to come face-to-face with pain and suffering. You will have to look at pictures, rehash testimony, and try to capture a sense of Mr. Jones's suffering in order to do justice here today.

- Members of the jury, you have the power here today to determine whether Ms. Smith will ever recover anything for this incident. There will not be another jury that will have that power. Your decision today is the final word as to what Ms. Smith will ever get. If you give nothing, that is exactly what Ms. Smith will ever get, nothing. A famous person once said: "I can't do everything, but I must do what I can." You, the jury, cannot cure Ms. Smith. You do not have the ability to make everything the same as it was. But you do have the ability to do the best you can for Ms. Smith. You have the ability to provide the means for Ms. Smith to get proper medical care, proper modifications to her home so she can get around, appropriate transportation, and the ability to go to a movie or a restaurant. You have the ability to allow Ms. Smith to live the most normal life she will ever be able to. You have a tremendous responsibility today. You may be thinking, "Why did I get involved in this? Why me? Out of all of the people in this county, why did I get picked?" I can't answer that question. I cannot tell you what fate brought you and Ms. Smith together, but you are here. All I ask you is that you return a just and fair result.

*Pain and Suffering: Cases Involving Young Adults*

- The Plaintiff in this case is only nineteen years old. He has sixty more years of life. To give you an idea of how long that is, sixty years ago it was the year 1942. Since 1942, we have had World War II (1941). The Korean Conflict (1950). The Bay of Pigs invasion in Cuba (1961). The Vietnam War (1964) and the Gulf War (1990). President Harry Truman (1945). President Dwight Eisenhower (1953). President John F. Kennedy (1960). President Lyndon Johnson (1963). President Richard Nixon (1968). President Gerald Ford (1974). President Jimmy Carter (1976). President Ronald Reagan (1980). President George Bush (1988). President Bill Clinton (1992), and President George Bush, also known as "W" (2000). Jackie Robinson was the first African-American to play professional baseball (1945). McCarthy Red Scare (1950). Civil Rights Movement (1960). Kennedy assassination (1963). Martin Luther King assassination (1968). Bobby Kennedy assassination. (1968). First astronauts land on the moon (1969). Watergate (1973). John Lennon assassinated (1980). President Reagan shot (1981). Challenger explosion (1986). World Trade Centers were attacked and destroyed, leaving three thousand people dead (2001).

- Ms. Jones has sixty more years of life according to the mortality tables. Therefore, in the year 2062, she will still be alive. While most of the people sitting in this courtroom today will likely have passed on, the decision you make today will determine what Ms. Jones' life will be like the year 2062 and what her life will be like for every year leading up to 2062. Your decision will determine whether she will live off government programs and be unable to select where she lives and who will provide her health care and personal care, or whether she will be able to select her own living arrangements with proper accommodations for her disabilities and with proper health care and personal care.

*Pain and Suffering: Soft-Tissue Injuries*

- One small scratch in an album, even if it only occurs intermittently in the album, can destroy the entire album.

- One small pebble in a shoe can cause an individual to not be able to perform any activities involving walking and can cause enough pain to prevent most other activities.

- A small piece of glass located in an automobile tire can bring a 4,000-pound vehicle to a complete stop and render it useless.

- A 10% impairment means that a man who is operating at 90% has to compete for jobs with people who are operating at 100%.

- A clock with a 5% impairment loses over one hour every day.

*Loss of Enjoyment of Life*

- One thing that experience has unfortunately taught all of us is that at times we are all guilty of taking everything that is important to us for granted. The truth is that the very things that bring us the most happiness, the most quality to our lives, are the things we take absolutely for granted every day.

We do not get up each day and feel blessed that we are able to see, hear, think, smell, taste, talk, feel, walk, run, drive, work, and play. We expect all of this. We demand all of this. We feel cheated if we are denied any of this.

We train our minds to believe that we are entitled to these things that truly add real quality to our lives, and we train our minds to believe that we will always have them. You know why this belief, this habit of taking these things for granted, is so much a part of our mindset; why it is such a part of the way we live day to day? Because it is too horrible, too painful, to ever imagine a life without these things. It is unbearable to think that one day we could wake up and no longer have them.

Most of the things we take for granted are simply so critical to our happiness, our enjoyment of life, that our mind does not want to focus on a life any other way. But when you go back into that jury room, part of your job will be to focus on those things on behalf of Mrs. Jacks. You will have to focus on how horrible it must be for Mrs. Jacks to have lost those things that she also likely took for granted, those things that added true enjoyment and quality to her life; and unfortunately those things she now realizes the importance.

There is a saying that the simple things in life are the most important. Unfortunately, it is tragedies such as this one that make us realize just how true this saying is, and why we should be grateful every second of every day.

## Chapter 7
## LAW ON CLOSING ARGUMENT

Traditionally, trial lawyers have considered closing argument a time to provide an unfettered dissertation as to why the jurors should find for their client. There were few boundaries, other than a lawyer was not permitted to ask the jurors to put themselves in the shoes of the client. This was considered a violation of The "Golden Rule" and often resulted in reversal.

Recently, trial and appellate courts have been much more willing to reverse a jury verdict based on statements made during closing argument. Often the courts find that the lawyer violated Rule 3.4(e) of the *Model Rules of Professional Conduct*. This rule provides that a lawyer shall not:

> in trial, allude to any matter that the lawyer does not reasonably believe is relevant or that will not be supported by admissible evidence, assert personal knowledge of facts in issue except when testifying as a witness, or state a personal opinion as to the justness of a cause, the credibility of a witness, the culpability of a civil litigant, or the guilt or innocence of an accused.

In an effort to demonstrate some of the potential boundaries in closing argument, and the statements that can result in a mistrial or reversal, the authors provide an extensive list of cases throughout the country addressing specific closing arguments.

The cases below are not considered to be an exhaustive search of state law. Moreover, considering how quickly state law changes, it is very likely that many of the cases below have now been reversed or altered by subsequent decisions. The decisions below are thus not meant to be cited in briefs to the court, but simply to give you a very good idea of the variety of decisions on closing argument statements, and to provide a starting point for researching the law.

Based on the decisions below, the best policy is to object to improper closing argument as it occurs and seek a curative instruction. Also, ask the court to take a motion for new trial under advisement. If a lawyer does not take each of these steps during the closing argument, the attorney may waive his right to appeal the improper remarks.

## Court Decisions

*Aetna Cas. and Surety Co. v. Kaufman,* 463 So.2d 520 (Fla. 3d DCA 1985): New trial ordered where defense counsel stated "I added all this up at $461,775 and the only thing I see is [plaintiff's counsel] getting rich."

*Allen v. State,* 662 So.2d 323, 328 (Fla. 1995): "To preserve an allegedly improper prosecutorial comment for review, a defendant must object to the comment and move for a mistrial." "The defendant cannot complain about the prosecutor's comments when defense counsel emphasized the same information to the jury as part of the defense strategy."

*Allstate Ins. Co. v. Wood,* 535 So.2d 699 (Fla. 1st DCA 1988): Reference to insurance may be rendered harmless by a trial court curative instruction to the jury.

*Alvarez v. State,* 574 So.2d 1119, 1120-21 (Fla. 3d DCA 1991): Personal attack upon accused, his defense, or his counsel is reversible error.

*Ballard v. American Land Cruisers, Inc.*, 537 So.2d 1018 (3d DCA 1988), rev. denied, 545 So.2d 1366 (Fla. 1989): Damage award of $50,000 for mother's mental pain and suffering caused by child's death in motor vehicle accident in which child's father was driving was grossly insufficient, and was explainable only as a result of prejudicial impact of father's counsel's repeated references to the tortfeasor's remorse and inference that father would bear burden of any damage award, which was not true, as the father was insured.

*Baptist Hospital v. Rawson*, 674 So.2d 777 (Fla. 1st DCA 1996): Arguments in derogation of Rule 3.4(e) that are so pervasive as to affect the fairness of the proceeding will not be condoned even in the absence of objection. Counsel's comments that defendants were idiots and defense was ridiculous and comments that defense was insulting to jury's intelligence and that counsel did not understand the defense were reversible error.

*Bloch v. Addis*, 493 So.2d 539 (Fla. 3d DCA 1986): New trial ordered where plaintiff's counsel stated that defendant's expert prepared his notes in the hall and was part of the same country club as the defendant. There was no evidence to support either one of these statements.

*Blue Grass Shows, Inc. v. Collins*, 614 So.2d 626 (1st DCA), cert. denied, 624 So.2d 264 (Fla. 1993): "We view, with some skepticism, appellant's agonized cries that comments by opposing counsel deprived him of a fair and impartial trial, when not so much as an objection was deemed necessary upon the occasion of the supposedly fatal utterances. We must assume that silence from experienced counsel is a judgment play predicated on his or her concept of how the trial is going. As such the failure to object constitutes intentional trial tactics, mistakes of which are not to be corrected on appeal simply because they backfire, save in most rare of circumstances." Additionally, plaintiff's counsel's "conscience of the community" argument at closing in negligence suit, while improper, did not warrant reversal absent objection, particularly as counsel did not follow improper remark with suggestion or request that jury should punish defendant.

*Borden, Inc. v. Young,* 479 So.2d 850 (3d DCA 1985), *rev. denied,* 488 So.2d 832 (Fla. 1986): A new trial was ordered when plaintiff's counsel stated: "Borden, you know with all your resources and all of your assets and everything that you got—you have tried to destroy this family, you have put resources behind your defense that are unreal. They have done things that you can't possibly imagine and Eddie is supposed to be able to go in and counteract this type of resources. It's absolutely and totally impossible. They say, but don't hold it against us. Don't hold it against Elsie. Well, I got to tell you something. Elsie isn't the sweet little cow you see on the milk can. Obviously, Elsie is a great big corporation and they are there to do one thing, lay it off on somebody else to take care of this man and this lady for the rest of their lives, lay it off on anybody you can lay it off to."

*Bosch v. Hajjar,* 639 So.2d 1096, 1097-98 (Fla. 4th DCA 1994): Defense counsel's improper expression of personal opinion and citations of facts outside the record in violation of Rule 3.4(e) not reversible because plaintiff's counsel did not object. "A proper and timely objection would have afforded the trial judge an opportunity to give a curative instruction and remove the prejudice created by appellee's trial counsel."

*Boutte v. Winn-Dixie Louisiana, Inc.,* 674 So.2d 299 (La.App.3 Cir. 1996): Closing argument by counsel for supermarket, in slip and fall action brought by patron who was injured in supermarket, that finding of liability by jury would cause cost of goods for supermarket's consumers, including jurors, to rise, was not supported by admissible evidence, and constituted deliberate resort to local prejudice, and so should not have been allowed. Insinuation by counsel that patron's medical treatment derived from some "medical/legal machine," rather than from her legitimate needs, was not supported by admissible evidence, but rather was unduly prejudicial by shrouding patron's case in anti-lawyer sentiments and averting jury from deciding case before it solely on merits, and so was improper.

*Brumage v. Pulmer*, 502 So.2d 966 (3d DCA), rev. denied, 513 So.2d 1062 (Fla. 1987): A "send them a message" type argument was not reversible error where no contemporaneous objection was made.

*Budget Rent A Car Systems, Inc. v. Jana*, 600 So.2d 466 (4th DCA), *rev. denied*, 606 So.2d 1165 (Fla. 1992): It was improper for counsel to refer to other side's expert as a "hired gun."

*Carnival Cruise Lines v. Rosania*, 546 So.2d 736 (Fla. 3d DCA 1989): The closing argument, "think about how Carnival Cruise Lines defended this particular case," warranted reversal in view of timely objection. Plaintiff's counsel also stated: "I didn't let Mr. Rosania testify....All he would testify to is he and his wife had a good family life beforehand."

*Cohen v. Pollack*, 674 So.2d 805 (Fla. 3d DCA 1996): It was improper for plaintiff's counsel to state: "How do you judge these damages? Let's start with pain and suffering. Like [Brittany] felt when [her doctor] operated on her or while she was at home for three weeks in agony, or most importantly, when these headaches keep coming and coming each day, each month. Try this. If a dentist told you he's got to do a root canal and he's only going to charge five dollars for the root canal and ninety-five dollars for the Novocain, you would pay that ninety-five dollars." Counsel also stated: "she [appellees' witness] told the truth," "everything we told you is true," and "everything we've been telling you about Brittany Pollack, every single last detail is true." Counsel also stated: "[appellants' counsel] and his witnesses will say anything," "he had to create a defense," and "he can't even tell the truth about a picture staring at him....How can he continue to misrepresent things to the jury." A new trial was granted.

*Commonwealth v. Best*, 740 N.E.2d 1065 (Mass.App.Ct. 2001): Even if prosecutor indicated during closing argument that it was jury's job to return a verdict of guilty, such isolated comment did not require reversal of defendant's conviction for the distribution of heroin in light of the strength of the Commonwealth's case.

*Commonwealth v. Monzon*, 51 Mass.App.Ct. 245, 744 N.E.2d 1131 (2001): Prosecutor's remark during closing argument that child's foster mother was "as close to a saint as anyone we can produce in court" was not reversible error, as jury was capable of sorting out excessive claims.

*Craig v. State*, 510 So.2d 857, 865 (Fla. 1987), *cert. denied*, 108 S.Ct. 732 (1988): "When counsel refers to a witness or a defendant as being a 'liar,' and it is understood from the context that the charge is made with reference to testimony given by the person thus characterized, the prosecutor is merely submitting to the jury a conclusion that he is arguing can be drawn from the evidence. It was for the jury to decide what evidence and testimony was worthy of belief and the prosecutor was merely submitting his view of the evidence to them for consideration. There was no impropriety."

*Cummins Ala., Inc. v. Allbritten*, 548 So.2d 258 (1st DCA), *rev. denied*, 553 So.2d 1164 (Fla. 1989): It was not improper for defense counsel to ask jurors "to judge them in light of what you would have done as reasonable people."

*D'Auria v. Allstate Ins. Co.*, 673 So.2d 147 (Fla. 5th DCA 1996): Defense counsel engaged in character assassinations upon the plaintiff, plaintiff's counsel, and plaintiff's witnesses. Counsel repeatedly injected his personal opinions as to the credibility of the witnesses, belittled the plaintiff, appealed to the conscience of the jurors to send a message to the community, and apologized to the jury for the plaintiff's case.

However, because there was no objection and motion for mistrial, a new trial was denied.

*Davis v. State*, 604 So.2d 794, 797 (Fla. 1992): Prosecutor stated "it might not be a bad idea to look at [the knife] and think about what it would feel like if it was two inches into your neck." Although comment was improper "golden rule," it was not reversible because it occurred at the end of lengthy and otherwise unemotional closing argument.

*Deck's Inc. v. Nunez*, 299 So.2d 165 (2d DCA 1974), *cert. denied*, 308 So.2d 112 (Fla. 1975): It is improper to suggest that the jury award enough to cover plaintiff's attorney's fees.

*Degren v. State*, 352 Md. 400, 722 A.2d 887 (Maryland 1999): Allowing prosecutor to tell jury in closing argument that the "number one reason" for not believing what defendant said was that "nobody in this country has more reason to lie than a defendant in a criminal trial" was not error where comment was in response to an attack on credibility of witnesses first raised by defense counsel in his closing argument.

*Devlin v. State*, 674 So.2d 795 (Fla. 5th DCA 1996): A new trial was denied despite the prosecutor's making the following statements in closing argument: "She's a good cop and she's an honest cop. She's an honest investigator." "And I can tell you something, that based on the evidence and the law, I want to just tell you, I submit to you that a not guilty verdict would be contrary to the law and would not be a verdict that speaks the truth."

*Donahue v. FPA Corporation*, 677 So.2d 882 (Fla. 4th DCA 1996): Defense counsel violated Rule 3.4(e) when he compared an expert video to the 20/20 video on GMC trucks blowing up and when he compared an expert to lawyers who advertise on benches 1-800-SUE. However, because statements were not objected to and were not fundamental error, no new trial granted.

*Dutcher v. Allstate Ins.*, 655 So.2d 1217 (Fla. 4th DCA 1995): It was improper for counsel to state: "He would like you to think that Dr. Routman is in my hip pocket, but he's been in cases against me. He's a good doctor. He's not on any side. He calls it like it is, and I think you will see that for yourself." "I don't think there is a chiropractor that would ever stop someone from having more care....Folks, asking a chiropractor to cut off another chiropractor is sort of like throwing kerosene on a fire."

*Eastern S.S. Lines, Inc. v. Martial*, 380 So.2d 1070 (3d DCA), *cert. denied*, 388 So.2d 1115 (Fla. 1980): Plaintiff's counsel's statement that "I went to Vietnam and I thought I had seen it all" required new trial.

*Esty v. State*, 642 So.2d 1074, 1079 (Fla. 1994), *cert. denied*, 115 S.Ct. 1380 (1995): Prosecutor's comment that defendant was a "dangerous, vicious, cold-blooded murderer" and prosecutor's "warning" to the jury that neither the police nor judicial system can "protect us from people like that" not so prejudicial as to vitiate the entire trial, even though defendant objected and moved for mistrial.

*Fant-Caughman v. State*, 61 S.W.3d 25 (Tex. App. 2001): Prosecutor's improper statement in closing argument that "I could have been here with witnesses for several more days, because there are a lot of people who know about these allegations" constituted reversible error since statement was calculated to cause jury to consider witnesses whose testimony was not admitted into evidence; trial court did not attempt to cure this improper jury argument; and evidence regarding the penetration of the victim, an essential element of the crime, was equivocal.

*Fayden v. Guerrero*, 474 So.2d 320 (Fla. 3d DCA 1985): Court ordered new trial where plaintiff's counsel argued that the defendants "should not have defended against the plaintiff's action but rather should have gone to the plaintiff and put $6,000,000 down on the table for her."

*Florida Crushed Stone Co. v. Johnson*, 546 So.2d 1102, 1104 (Fla. 5th DCA 1989): Plaintiff's counsel's "conscience of the community" argument at closing in negligence suit was not improper as counsel did not follow improper remark with suggestion or request that jury should punish defendant.

*Forman v. Wallshein*, 671 So.2d 872 (Fla. 3d DCA 1996): Counsel is permitted to call witnesses "liars" if the evidence supports the statements. Also, counsel's statements "I believe" and "I think" were merely figures of speech and not improper.

*Fowler v. N. Goldring Corp.*, 582 So.2d 802 (Fla. 1st DCA 1991): Defense counsel's statement that plaintiff was seeking the "New American Dream" by seeking money in a personal injury lawsuit was reversible error.

*Fravel v. Haughey*, 727 So.2d 1033 (Fla. 5th DCA 1999): Although comments made by plaintiff's counsel during closing argument, including comments requesting jury to act as conscious of community and accusing defendant, his attorney and witnesses of perjury, were improper and inflammatory, no new trial in absence of timely objection.

*Ganesan v. State*, 45 S.W.3d 197 (Tex. App. 2001): Prosecutor's erroneous statements that "if you acquit that man, you are signing those two women's death warrants" and "you will be signing the death warrants of those two young women if you acquit this man," although highly inflammatory, did not require reversal where remarks did not violate mandatory statute or inject new facts into case.

*Gardner v. State*, 792 So.2d 1000 (Miss. App. 2001): The prosecutor made the following statement in closing argument: "Think about it. Take control of the situation. Take your town back." Defense counsel objected. The trial judge sustained the objection and made the following order: "The jury will disregard the last comment by the prosecutor. Ladies and Gentlemen: You've got to make your decision from the evidence and the law and that alone." During a recess that immediately followed the closing statements, Gardner made a motion for a mistrial based on the "take your town back" comment made by the state. The court concluded that the natural and probable effect of the improper argument did not create an unjust prejudice against the accused as to result in a decision influenced by the prejudice.

*George v. Mann*, 622 So.2d 151 (Fla. 3d DCA 1993): Defense counsel's references to plaintiff's "lawsuit pain" and suggestion that plaintiff "set up" lawsuit, and implying that plaintiff was a liar who was perpetrating a fraud and concealing evidence, was reversible error even though there was no objection.

*Goff v Ontario Ltd.*, 539 So.2d 1158 (Fla. 3d DCA 1989): New trial ordered where defense counsel stated that VA hospital "doesn't cost them anything" due to plaintiff's military veteran status. Motion for mistrial not required to preserve issue on appeal.

*Goodin v. State*, 787 So.2d 639 (Miss. 2001): Statement by prosecutor at sentencing stage of capital murder case that victim did not have the protection of the law that defendant had received did not require reversal of death sentence in view of overwhelming evidence of defendant's callous indifference to human life.

*Grau v. Branham*, 761 So.2d 375 (Fla. 4th DCA 2000): Counsel objected to opposing counsel's repeated references to a treatise as a "Nazi" source. Counsel objected, but did not move for a mistrial or seek a curative instruction. "Our court has all but closed the door on fundamental error in civil trials." The attorney made a tactical decision in not requesting a curative instruction and not moving for a mistrial. "The trial court was in a much better vantage point than we are in determining whether the comments vitiated the fairness of the trial and, as such, we must affirm."

*Harne v. Deadmond*, 287 Mont. 255, 954 P.2d 732, 1998 MT 22 (1998): Attorney vouching for credibility of his client by telling jury in closing argument about his own favorable experience with client violated rule of professional conduct, and required a new trial where court did not admonish or otherwise instruct jury not to consider improper arguments.

*Hawk v. State*, 718 So.2d 159 (Fla. 1998): No abuse of discretion in instructing jury to disregard comment regarding "amoral, vicious, cold-blooded killer." Comments regarding "taking life for granted" and "savage killer" not preserved for appellate review. Comment regarding "insult to all who have achieved greatness" was inappropriate but not reversible.

*Hayden v. Elam*, 739 So.2d 1088 (Ala. 1999): Statement in closing argument referencing the "under penalty of perjury language" in tax return was improper. However, new trial was not warranted where defendant timely objected, trial court gave curative instruction, defendant made no further objection, and defendant did not move for mistrial.

*Hobson v. State*, 675 N.E.2d 1090 (Ind. 1996): Defendant failed to show that prosecutor improperly gave personal opinion in calling witnesses liars. Comment merely pointed out incongruities in testimony presented at trial, concluding that someone must not be testifying truthfully and inviting jury to determine which witness was telling the truth.

*Jackson v. State*, 690 So.2d 714 (Fla. 4th DCA 1997): Prosecutor's comments in closing argument implying that defendant was a drug dealer were improper where defendant was charged with possession, not sale, of marijuana and cocaine. State's closing highly inflammatory where prosecutor argued that drugs are the "root of all crime" and that the jury had defendant to "thank for all that." Trial court abused discretion in denying motion for mistrial.

*Jackson Memorial Hosp. v. Geter*, 613 So.2d 126 (Fla. 3d DCA 1993): It was improper for counsel to argue that jury should place monetary value on the life of plaintiff's decedent in the same way value is placed on a "Boeing 747 or a SCUD missile."

*Kendall Skating Centers, Inc. v. Martin*, 448 So.2d 1137 (Fla. 3d DCA 1984): Calling defendants "despicable" and their lawyers "liars" mandated reversal.

*Klose v. Choy*, 673 So.2d 81 (Fla. 4th DCA 1996): It was improper for defense counsel to argue in closing argument that adverse medical malpractice verdict would impact the reputation of the defendant doctor.

*Knepper v. Genstar Corp.*, 537 So.2d 619 (3d DCA 1988), *rev. denied*, 545 So.2d 1367 (Fla. 1989): New trial ordered where plaintiff's counsel stressed defendant's Canadian background and asked the jury to send a message to Canada. Court stated counsel tried to incite the prejudice of the American jury.

*Laberg v. Vancleave*, 534 So.2d 1176 (Fla. 5th DCA 1988): Defense counsel is not permitted to say that plaintiff's counsel always asks for ten times more than what he is seeking.

*Lowder v. Economic Opportunity Family Health Center*, 680 So.2d 1133 (Fla. 3d DCA 1996): Counsel not permitted to argue for an adverse inference that a witness was not called when witness was equally available to both parties. The witness was a former employee, not a present employee, and the witness' testimony was cumulative, and there was a valid explanation as to why the witness could not be called. Also, phrases such as "I think," "I believe," and "I disagree" are figures of speech and do not constitute vouching or expressions of personal opinion.

*Martin v. State Farm Mut. Auto Ins. Co.*, 392 So.2d 11 (Fla. 5th DCA 1980): New trial ordered where defense counsel stated "but if you give her an award, then every time she spends those dollars she's going to think about this case, and I submit that's just too much for her to bear....I think that's what he's doing, selling beef."

*Mein, Joest & Hayes v. Weiss*, 516 So.2d 299 (Fla. 1st DCA 1987): New trial ordered where defense counsel referred to the "litigious plaintiffs."

*Metropolitan Dade County v. Cifuentes*, 473 So.2d 297 (Fla. 3d DCA 1985): Court ordered a new trial as a result of counsel's stating, "I know last night I did not sleep. I know that last night was probably the first time in a long time that I told my wife that I loved her. I know that I was in fear last night, not fear of dying but fear of living if someone I loved died."

*Miami Beach Texaco v. Price*, 433 So.2d 1227 (Fla. 3d DCA 1983): Defense counsel cannot comment that taxpayers will have to pay the award.

*Nastri v. Vermillion Bros., Inc.*, 46 Conn.Supp. 285, 747 A.2d 1069 (1998): Operator of tractor trailer promptly voiced objection to allegedly improper remarks at the end of the opposing counsel's closing argument, requested curative instruction, and excepted to the court's failure to give instruction. Such actions were sufficient to preserve for review, in motion to set aside the verdict, contention that opposing counsel's remarks deprived him of a fair trial.

*Owens Corning Fiberglass Corp. v. Crane*, 683 So. 2d 552 (Fla. 3d DCA 1996): Counsel impugning the credibility of the other party by accusing the party or counsel of fabricating evidence or misleading the jury is fundamental error.

*Parker v. Todd*, 695 So.2d 424 (Fla. 4th DCA 1997): It was improper for defense counsel to argue: "Our society is such that, for whatever reason, it seems that we've gotten to the point where every time something

140

happens, it has to be somebody's fault. Even criminals in courtrooms now blame the system, their parents' upbringings, their schooling; it's somebody else's fault." "We find the remarks to be also improper because they referred to matters outside of the evidence. Reference to 'criminals' not accepting responsibility for their actions simply had no place in this lawsuit. By conjuring up distasteful images of society's ills from frivolous lawsuits to the refusal to take responsibility for one's own actions, these remarks diverted the jury's attention from the issues it should have been deciding."

*Parker v. State,* 641 So.2d 369, 375 (Fla. 1994), *cert. denied,* 115 S.Ct. 944 (1995): Prosecutor's statement that defense counsel's argument was "fantasy" was not reversible error as the statement was fair comment on, and perhaps invited by, defendant's closing.

*People v. Knapp,* 244 Mich. App. 361, 624 N.W.2d 227 (2001): Reversal of conviction for second-degree criminal sexual conduct was not warranted for prosecutor's vouching for victim's credibility at closing argument. Defendant failed to object, a curative instruction would have removed any taint, and jury was instructed that lawyers' arguments were not evidence.

*Pippin v. Latosynski,* 622 So.2d 566 (Fla. 1st DCA 1993): Counsel is not permitted to comment on the amount of money spent by other side in defending itself, and cannot ask the jury to send a message to a non-party witness.

*Russell, Inc. v. Trento,* 445 So.2d 390 (Fla. 3d DCA 1984): New trial ordered where plaintiff's counsel stated that he had lived with the case and represented the plaintiff for three years and had carried the burden for three years in representing the family. Counsel also stated, "In our society, we value life very preciously....You six people have the ultimate say-so on what a life is worth and what [the deceased's] life was worth to

Mrs. Trento." The court found that the value of human life is not an element of damages under Florida law.

*S. H. Investment and Develop. Corp. v. Kincaid*, 495 So.2d 768 (5th DCA), *rev. denied*, 504 So.2d 767 (Fla. 1987): Court ordered a new trial when plaintiff's counsel stated, "If you weren't as incensed by what you heard as I was as I began to uncover the facts of this case, if you're not upset, if you're not bothered by the conduct of these corporations and the absolute insensitivity they have to people's rights and something that they hold so dearly as a home, then I have failed you and I have failed my clients. Never have I seen so much evidence; never have I seen so many strong fingers of guilt pointing to the culpable parties." Plaintiff's counsel also stated that his client's statements were true, honest and candid.

*Sacred Heart Hospital v. Stone*, 650 So.2d 676 (1st DCA), *rev. denied*, 659 So.2d 1089 (Fla. 1995): New trial granted where plaintiff's counsel contended that the defense's theory was "ridiculous," where counsel informed the jury that his client had told him that he believed one of the defense experts was lying, where counsel said, "I think he did an exceptional job," and where counsel told the jury to deal "very, very harshly" with defendants. New trial granted even though defendant did not object or raise issues in motion for new trial.

*Sanchez v. State*, 792 So.2d 286 (Miss. App. 2001): Prosecutor's conjecture during closing argument that those who commit predatory crimes use alcohol or marijuana as an excuse for their acts did not constitute reversible error, where prosecutor clarified to jury that he was in no way asserting that the defendant had been using marijuana.

*Schubert v. Allstate Ins. Co.*, 603 So.2d 554 (5th DCA), *rev. dismissed*, 606 So.2d 1164 (Fla. 1992): Defense counsel's statement that plaintiff's doctor always found a permanent impairment, plaintiff was seeking a large fortune, plaintiff's child is going to think that a lawsuit is the way to get ahead, that plaintiff should be thankful he wasn't injured more seriously, that defense counsel was telling the truth, and that plaintiff's counsel would do anything to advance his cause was reversible error even without objection.

*Shaffer v. Ward,* 510 So.2d 602 (Fla. 5th DCA 1987): It was not fundamental error when the jury was asked to place themselves in a non-financial responsibility position like client's. Defense counsel stated that "everyone has had a close call driving, close calls don't mean you're negligent. It was a close call because the car in front of you unexpectedly stopped." Defense counsel also stated, "you all drive. You know the importance of brake lights."

*Silva v. Nightingale,* 619 So.2d 4 (Fla. 5th DCA 1993): Counsel's statement that he did not believe plaintiff, and that jury should disregard plaintiff's testimony, and that chiropractors give permanent impairment more readily than other doctors was reversible even though plaintiff's counsel did not object.

*Simmons v. Swinton,* 715 So.2d 370 (Fla. 5th DCA 1998): Defense counsel stated that the plaintiff's treating physician had self-interested motives in assigning plaintiff a permanent impairment rating, and stated that "based on his care, we know that he was negligent." Defense counsel made numerous statements that alluded to matters not in evidence and made statements of personal opinions as to the credibility of witnesses. New trial was denied because plaintiff failed to object and such failure was a tactical decision.

*Simmons v. Lowrey,* 563 So.2d 183 (Fla. 4th DCA 1990): It was not impermissible "golden rule" argument for plaintiff's counsel to ask the jury as they listened to the case "to think about what you would pay someone for one day of what you will hear she has to go through for the rest of her life."

*State v. Pabst*, 268 Kan. 501, 996 P.2d 321 (2000): Prosecutor's improper remarks during closing argument, including his accusing defendant of lying, coupled with trial court's overruling defendant's timely objection, denied defendant a fair trial and required a reversal.

*State v. Hazley*, 19 P.3d 800 (Kan. App. 2001): Prosecutor's comments during closing argument expressing personal opinion on credibility of sole defense witness, focusing on post-Miranda silence of same witness, and inaccurately accusing defense attorney of arguing that officer who conducted search leading to present charges had lied during his testimony, denied defendant a fair trial and constituted reversible error.

*State v. Magdaleno*, 17 P.3d 974 (Kan. App. 2001): Prosecutor's statements during closing argument, labeling defense counsel a liar by saying she had "argue[d] facts that she knows [aren't] true" and making other similar statements, reflected ill will on the part of prosecutor toward defendant and was gross and flagrant misconduct, and constituted reversible error.

*State v. Pouncey*, 241 Conn. 802, 699 A.2d 901 (1997): Prosecutor's improper comments during closing argument that victims "were confronted with what suburbanites would call the ultimate urban nightmare," and that victims "were in the wrong place at the wrong time in an urban neighborhood," were not so offensive as to have had bearing on jury's verdict. The objectionable remarks were brief, isolated, and not so prejudicial as to prompt immediate objection by defendant. There was no evidence that comments were product of deliberate appeal by prosecutor to racial biases or stereotypes, reversal would have forced victims to relive emotional trauma they suffered as result of attack, and potential for memory loss by victims and witnesses was legitimate concern given lapse of time from incident.

*State v. Bureau*, 134 N.H. 220, 589 A.2d 1013 (1991): Prosecutor did not improperly vouch for credibility of victim during closing argument by referring to victim's testimony as "the truth." Defense counsel had continually attacked victim's credibility by stating that victim's testimony "just didn't make sense."

*State v. Satchwell,* 244 Conn. 547, 710 A.2d 1348 (1998): Defendant was not entitled to new trial based on prosecutor's improper closing remarks suggesting that redacted transcript pages of plea hearing were relevant to case. Defendant promptly objected to the remarks, and trial court immediately instructed jury to disregard remarks. Defendant made no claim at trial, and made no claim on appeal, that cautionary instruction given to jury was incomplete or otherwise defective, and prosecutor promptly apologized for his comments.

*State v. Oehman,* 212 Conn. 325, 562 A.2d 493 (1989): Prosecutor's comment during closing argument that defendant was a "spoiled killer with a gun" was an improper statement. However, such statement did not deny defendant a fair trial in a murder case, where comment was not part of a pattern of strident and repeated misconduct. Prosecutor's comments during closing argument characterizing defendant as a liar, coward, and person without principles were supported by the evidence presented and did not deny defendant a fair trial. Prosecutor's comments during closing argument concerning his belief in credibility of various state witnesses, although improper, did not deny defendant a fair trial. Comments were made immediately prior to the attorney's recapitulation of the witness testimony, and were not part of pattern of prosecutorial misconduct.

*State v. Lafferty,* 20 P.3d 342, 368, 415 Utah Adv. Rep. 29 (2001): In a particularly gruesome murder trial, prosecutor said the following: "Erica Lafferty, Brenda and Allen's daughter, would have turned 13 years old this year; in fact, this month....When baby Erica showed up on this man's death list it told you more about his character than all the witnesses, all the friends and acquaintances, all the experts that the defense called on his behalf. It demonstrated a blatant and callous disregard for life, for innocent human life. And if for no other reason, justice demands that Erica's murder result in punishment, too. If you determine that the defendant deserves life without parole before we even consider Erica lying dead in her crib, before we ever consider that the second person he killed was a 15-month-old infant, then there's only one punishment left that is meaningful, and that is death." The court held that the prosecutor's comments did not constitute victim impact evidence. The information did not tell [the jury] about her character, the impact the death had on her family, or her family's opinions about the crime. Additionally, these details were already properly admitted at trial. Court noted that a prosecutor has the right to draw inferences and use the information brought out at trial in his closing argument.

*Stokes v. Wet N' Wild,* 523 So.2d 181 (Fla. 5th DCA 1988): New trial granted where defense counsel stated: "I don't mean to insult your intelligence and please excuse me if I do. This adds up to $48,300 and it is absolutely ridiculous. This is why we're here. This is why our courtrooms are crowded and this is why we read articles in the newspaper, because of things like that."

*Tito v. Potshnick,* 488 So.2d 100 (4th DCA), *rev. denied,* 494 So.2d 1152 (Fla. 1986): New trial ordered where defense argued, "I think each and everyone knows that this young lady is an attractive young lady, that this boy is going to have a father....This boy is going to have a father sometime in the future. There is no doubt [of] that as attractive as she is."

*Trump v. State,* 753 A.2d 963 (Del. Supr. 2000): Prosecutor's closing argument stating, "I submit to you" that the child victim of sexual assault was telling the truth was improper vouching for the credibility of a witness.

*Venet v. Garcia*, 433 So.2d 53 (Fla. 3d DCA 1983): It was improper for defense counsel to state "but for the Grace of God all of us would be in this position."

*Wilbur v. Calvin Hightower*, 778 So.2d 381 (Fla. 4th DCA 2001): Plaintiff's argument referring to the price of paintings sold at auction was not an argument that jury should place monetary value on decedent's life, but rather on her surviving spouse's loss. Thus, argument was proper.

*Williams v. State*, 911 S.W.2d 788 (Tex. App. 1995): Prosecutor's statement to the jury that it should "ask defense to at least present you with a consistent defense" was not extreme or manifestly improper, and did not inject new and harmful facts into evidence, and thus was not reversible error where instruction in court's charge clearly set out the burden of proof.

## Chapter 8
## CONCLUDING REMARKS

The authors of this book are of different ages ranging from thirty-eight to sixty-five. All three come from substantially different generational perspectives when it comes to defining what good advocacy should look and sound like. They each, however, have been highly successful trial lawyers by believing in, and abiding by, the following ideas regarding improving advocacy skills:

- Becoming a proficient trial lawyer requires that we all do our best to round our lives out as much as possible. As trial lawyers, we must all be capable of accurately understanding the life experiences of people regardless of their race, religion, gender, social status, and economic status. We must accept the fact that if we expect to share wisdom, compassion, and understanding with a jury in our closing arguments, then we must constantly be growing in these areas 365 days a year.

- Every day in our lives there is something occurring around us—an event, a statement, a story, perhaps even a mundane routine—that should arm us with effective, richer ideas for advocacy if we are in the habit of paying attention. If we are unable to take a stroll through a neighborhood on a Saturday afternoon and find a closing concept as we observe children playing, families interacting, and all of life's activities taking place before our very eyes, then perhaps trial advocacy is not our best calling. Everyday life experiences will lay claim to our best ideas. We must get in the habit of observing and recording these concepts when they occur.

- Trial lawyers should keep a file on closing ideas that have been a work in progress throughout their lawyering careers. The file can range from something that is superbly organized to something that looks like nothing more than a collection of notes and memos written on single sheets of legal paper and bar napkins stuffed into a manila folder. These files of closing concepts should be a collection of ideas that have been passed down from generations of other lawyers. They should be concepts that have been borrowed from war stories, seminars, newspapers, magazine articles, books, and years of trial experience.

- Exceptional trial lawyers do not simply borrow closing argument concepts from other lawyers and regurgitate them. Great trial lawyers utilize closing argument concepts and then add the nuances of substance that fit into their courtroom demeanor. They improve upon the concepts by matching them with words that sound like they came from their own mouths. They write down variations of the concepts. They talk about the ideas with other lawyers throughout their years of lawyering. They improve the ideas to the point where they can readily be retrieved from their memory and their heart when needed. In politics, such a collection of ideas is called "talking points," and they often sound hollow and shallow. In a courtroom, a collection of ideas and concepts needs to be developed into something that sounds more like art, not sound bites.

- Dogged, uncompromising, arduous hard work in the preparation of every deposition, opening, direct, cross, and, most especially, closing, is basic and essential to success. It is unfortunate that in the last twenty years far too many experienced trial lawyers have conveyed a "shoot from the hip" style that worked for them from time to time. That shoot-from-the-hip cowboy style is simply no longer relevant to trial advocacy. Creative spontaneity is effective only when it is supported and driven by hours and hours of heavy lifting and preparation long before the trial ever takes place. You absolutely must be capable of understanding your case facts and case law better than your opposition. A disciplined, honest, and thorough evaluation of the strengths and weaknesses of your case requires tedious, hard work.

- Finally, and most important, you will never become a great trial lawyer unless you go to court. You will never grow as a trial lawyer unless you show a strong commitment to actively going to trial every chance you get. It is no secret among trial lawyers why some attorneys stay away from the courtroom. There is the fear of being rejected by the jury. There is the fear of being labeled as the loser, which might stifle the growth of a trial lawyer's career. If you find yourself in that position, you must overcome the fear of failure. In fact, you must specifically expose yourself to that risk of failure by going to trial even when you don't want to.

Like any book, there will likely be very few specific points from your reading of this book that you will recall one week from now. Hopefully, there will be one or more concepts that you will remember that will prove productive in your practice. However, if you remember nothing else, you should remember that the practice of trial law can be summed up in three words: duty, confidence, and endurance.

**Duty**: Trial lawyers have a duty to fight injustice, and often the only place this can be done is before a jury. As Martin Luther King, Jr., stated: "The greatest sin of our time is not the few who have destroyed, but the vast majority who have sat idly by."

**Confidence**: To be successful as a trial lawyer, you must be confident, because there will always be critics—judges, opposing counsel, clients, witnesses, experts, members of the venire, and even jurors. A great trial lawyer must have the strength and confidence to never waiver in his position, or else the critics will be proved correct.

> Bullfight critics row on row
> Crowd the vast arena full
> But only one man's there who knows
> And he's the man who fights the bull.

*Attributed to Garcia Lorca (1898-1936)*

**Endurance**: To be a successful trial lawyer you must have endurance. There are going to be defeats along the way, even in cases that you felt you should have won. There will be critics, and there will be second-guessing. However, one thing you can be assured of, and that is if you try hard enough and long enough, there will be some tremendous victories, and it only takes one for you to realize and understand why it is so important that trial lawyers exist, and why you should always be proud to state: "I am a trial lawyer."

> It is not the critic who counts: not the man who points out how the strong man stumbles or where the doer of deeds could have done better. The credit belongs to the man who is actually in the arena, whose face is marred by dust and sweat and blood, who strives valiantly, who errs and comes up short again and again, because there is no effort without error or shortcoming, but who knows the great enthusiasms, the great devotions, who spends himself for a worthy cause; who, at the best, knows, in the end, the triumph of high achievement, and who, at the worst, if he fails, at least he fails while daring greatly, so that his place shall never be with those cold and timid souls who knew neither victory nor defeat.

*Theodore Roosevelt*

151

## Appendix 1
## NEGLIGENT SALE OF AMMUNITION—
## $2.2 MILLION JURY VERDICT

### Issues Addressed:

- Liability for negligent sale of ammunition to a minor

- Apportionment of liability among negligent and intentional tortfeasors

- Wrongful death damages in a volatile marriage

- Wrongful death damages when decedent has a problem past

### IN THE CIRCUIT COURT IN AND FOR ESCAMBIA COUNTY, FLORIDA

SANDRA COKER, as personal
representative of the Estate
of BILLY WAYNE COKER,
   Plaintiff,
vs.                     CASE NO.: 91-5408-CA-01
WAL-MART STORES, INC.,   DIVISION: "F"
a foreign corporation,
   Defendant.

### Summary of Case

In 1990, Robin Archer worked for Trout Auto Parts in Pensacola, Florida. Archer's job performance was unsatisfactory, and he was ultimately fired at the suggestion of a co-worker named Dan Wells. Thereafter, Archer decided to have Wells killed, and on Thursday,

January 24, 1991, Archer persuaded his cousin, Patrick Bonifay, to perform the killing.

Bonifay was seventeen years old at the time. Archer planned for Bonifay to go to the Trout Auto Parts store on "W" Street in Pensacola just before midnight. Bonifay was to approach the outside service window and ask the sales clerk for a 1985 Nissan truck clutch disc. The clerk would have to go to the back of the store to determine whether this particular part was in stock. When the clerk left the counter, Bonifay was to climb through the service window, shoot the clerk, and rob the store. The killing/robbery was to occur at midnight on Friday, January 25, 1991, or Saturday, January 26, 1991, because the person Archer wanted killed would be working during those times.

Bonifay decided to perform the killing/robbery. However, Bonifay did not have a gun, a motor vehicle, or a driver's license, and thus needed assistance. Bonifay borrowed a pistol from Kelly Bland, an eighteen-year-old friend, and Bonifay happened to have one bullet that fit in the gun. Bonifay then persuaded Cliff Barth, age seventeen, to assist in the robbery, and Eddie Fordham, age eighteen, to drive Bonifay and Barth to the Trout Auto Parts store.

On Friday, January 25, 1991, Fordham, Barth, and Bonifay drove to the Trout Auto Parts store on "W" Street. It was close to midnight and Wells was working. Bonifay approached the outside service window, and Wells immediately became suspicious because Bonifay kept looking over his shoulder and was wearing gloves and a coat, even though it was not cold outside. Bonifay asked Wells for a 1985 Nissan truck part, but Wells decided not to leave the counter. Instead, Wells opened a catalog, acted like he was looking for the part, and told Bonifay the part was not in stock. Bonifay then left.

The next night, Saturday, January 26, 1991, Bonifay decided to attempt the killing/robbery again. At approximately 8:00 P.M.,

Fordham picked Bonifay up at Bonifay's home. As the two were traveling to Barth's home, Bonifay asked Fordham if he was old enough to buy ammunition, and Fordham (age eighteen) said yes. Bonifay and Fordham thought a person could purchase pistol ammunition at eighteen years of age. Bonifay told Fordham to pull into Kmart on Mobile Highway. Bonifay and Fordham attempted to purchase .32 pistol ammunition, but the sales clerk said the store did not have any in stock. Fordham asked how much the ammunition would have cost, and the clerk said approximately fourteen dollars. Bonifay said he did not have enough money, and Bonifay and Fordham proceeded to Barth's home.

When Bonifay and Fordham arrived at Barth's home, Barth was getting dressed. Bonifay and Fordham told Barth that they no longer had any ammunition and that they needed to go to Wal-Mart on Highway 29 to purchase some, and asked to borrow money. It is unclear what had happened to the single bullet Bonifay had in the gun on Friday night, but there was a strong indication at trial that Bonifay had shot the remaining bullet out of Fordham's car window after leaving Trout Auto Parts on Friday night.

Bonifay and Fordham arrived at the Wal-Mart store at approximately 8:35 P.M. The two minors went to the gun counter, and Bonifay asked the clerk for .32 pistol ammunition. The clerk on duty that night was Ken Powell. Mr. Powell was twenty-two years of age at the time and had been selling ammunition for only seven months and had very limited training in ammunition sales. Bonifay asked for the ammunition and handed the money to Fordham. Powell got the ammunition and went to hand it to Fordham, but Fordham told Powell to hand the ammunition to Bonifay, which Powell did.

Fordham and Bonifay purchased the ammunition and then returned to Barth's home. Barth got into Fordham's vehicle and noticed that Bonifay possessed a box of ammunition. Barth watched

Bonifay take ammunition out of the box and fully load the gun. Approximately three hours later, the minors drove to Trout Auto Parts on "W" Street. That night, however, Wells was not working, as he was ill. Instead, Billy Wayne Coker was filling in this one night for Wells. Coker would not have been working at this particular store any other night, as Coker was assigned to a Trout Auto Parts store at a different location.

Upon arriving at Trout Auto Parts, Bonifay walked up to the service window, and Coker was on the phone talking with a customer. Bonifay shot Coker in the back. Bonifay and Barth then climbed through the service window and Bonifay shot Coker in the chest. Bonifay and Barth robbed the store of approximately $2,100, and on the way out Bonifay shot Coker in the head two times. It was the last two shots that caused Coker's death. The first two shots were survivable. Before Bonifay shot Coker in the head, Coker pleaded for his life, stating that he had a wife and two children and provided the ages of the children. Bonifay turned to Coker and stated: "Fuck you, fuck your wife, and fuck your children." These were the last words Coker heard before Bonifay executed him.

Approximately two weeks after the killing/robbery, Bonifay, Barth, and Fordham were arrested. When Fordham was arrested he immediately gave a statement to the police stating that he and Bonifay had gone to Wal-Mart on Saturday, January 26, at approximately 9:00 P.M., and bought the ammunition. Fordham said the Wal-Mart store was located on Highway 29 in Pensacola, and the ammunition cost approximately fifteen dollars, which he paid for with cash. Based on this information, the state attorney went to Wal-Mart and retrieved a cash register receipt that confirmed the sale of .32 automatic pistol ammunition at 8:39 P.M. on Saturday, January 26, by a sales clerk by the name of Kenneth Powell, paid for with fifteen dollars cash. In fact, the cash register receipt specifically evidenced that the ammunition sold was .32 auto pistol ammunition manufactured by Federal Cartridge Company. This was the exact caliber and brand of ammunition used to kill Coker.

As a result of her husband's death, Sandra Coker filed a lawsuit against Wal-Mart alleging that Wal-Mart was negligent in violating 18 U.S.C. 922(b)(1), a federal criminal statute that prohibits the sale of pistol ammunition to persons less than twenty-one years of age. Wal-Mart moved to dismiss the complaint on the basis that Bonifay's act in killing Coker was an intervening criminal act and was unforeseeable as a matter of law. The motion to dismiss was granted, and Coker appealed the trial court decision to the First District Court of Appeal, which reversed the decision. The District Court concluded that 18 U.S.C. 922(b)(1) was enacted to prevent the exact type of harm that occurred in this case, and that Wal-Mart could not be heard to complain that the harm actually occurred. The District Court further held that the issue of proximate causation was an issue for the jury and remanded the case for trial. Wal-Mart appealed the District Court decision to the Florida Supreme Court, but the Court denied review, and the case was remanded for trial.

One of the issues at trial was the apportionment of responsibility between Wal-Mart and the non-party tortfeasors. Specifically, six names were placed on the verdict form—Wal-Mart, Archer, Bland, Barth, Bonifay and Fordham. The jury found Wal-Mart 35% liable for Coker's death, Archer 25% responsible, Bland 0% responsible, Barth 8% responsible, Bonifay 25% responsible, and Fordham 7% responsible. The jury awarded approximately $2.2 million dollars in damages. The trial judge reduced the verdict to approximately $900,000, based on Wal-Mart's 35% responsibility. Wal-Mart appealed, and we cross-appealed arguing that the non-party tortfeasors should not have appeared on the verdict form. The First District Court of Appeals and the Florida Supreme Court upheld the jury verdict, and reinstated the $2.2 million verdict plus post-trial interest, ruling that the verdict could not be reduced by the acts of intentional tortfeasors.

The following is the closing argument that was presented at trial.

### Closing Argument

May it please the Court, Wal-Mart, Mrs. Coker, and especially you, the ladies and gentlemen of the jury.

We're at the stage of this trial known as closing arguments, and this is the last time we get to speak with you. It's a chance for the lawyers to tell you what we believe the evidence was, what we believe the judge will instruct you the law is, and how we believe the evidence should be applied.

After closing argument, you will get to go back to the jury room and reach your verdict. To assist you, the judge is going to give you a verdict form, and it's going to be identical to this form.

The very first question on the verdict form is going to be: Was there negligence on the part of Wal-Mart Stores, Inc. through one or more of its employees which was a legal cause of the death of the decedent, Billy Wayne Coker? Yes or no. Therefore, the first question is really two parts, was there negligence on Wal-Mart and was it a legal cause of Wayne's death?

What is the first part? Was there negligence? All that means is did Wal-Mart violate federal law when they sold this ammunition to Larry Fordham and Pat Bonifay, and that's all it means. If you find that they violated federal law, then they were negligent as a matter of law.

So what is the law? The law is Title 18 United States Code Section 922(b)(1), and what that provides is that a licensed dealer, which Wal-Mart is, shall not sell or deliver any ammunition to any individual who the dealer knows or has reasonable cause to believe is less than eighteen years of age. And if the ammunition is other than ammunition for a shotgun or a rifle, meaning pistol, to any individual who the dealer knows or has reasonable cause to believe is less than twenty-one years of age, and as it says here, a violation of this statute is negligent. If you find that the person alleged to have been negligent violated the statute, such a person was negligent.

What does the statute mean? If Wal-Mart sold .32 auto pistol ammunition, the buyers of the ammunition had to be twenty-one years of age. Therefore, the first question in this case is: Did Wal-MartMart sell the ammunition? The evidence in this case is totally unrefuted. Everyone who has testified said they did not have any ammunition on Saturday night. They had to borrow money from Barth. They went to Wal-Mart around closing, and they bought .32 auto pistol ammunition. Eddie Fordham was arrested two weeks after this murder. He gave a recorded statement to Officer Tom O'Neal. Eddie told Officer O'Neal that he and Bonifay went to Wal-Mart on Highway 29 near closing, bought ammunition; it was around fifteen dollars. After that statement, Officer O'Neal recovered the gun and a box of ammunition from Kelly Bland. The ammunition was a box of Federal Cartridge .32 auto pistol ammunition. After that point, the state attorney went to the Wal-Mart on Highway 29 and got their cash register receipts for that night.

What does the receipt show? It shows that at 8:39 P.M., right before closing at nine o'clock, Wal-Mart sold .32 auto ammunition manufactured by Federal Cartridge Company and that fifteen dollars cash was used to pay for it.

The ammunition obviously came from Wal-Mart. In fact, what did Investigator Tom O'Neal testify to? He was the lead investigator in this murder case. He said there was absolutely no evidence of ammunition coming from anywhere other than Wal-Mart on Highway 29. What did Mike Patterson testify to? He's now the United States Attorney. At the time he was the state attorney who prosecuted all four boys. He testified that there was no evidence of ammunition coming from anywhere other than Wal-Mart on Highway 29.

What does Wal-Mart say? Wal-Mart says, "We didn't sell it. We absolutely did not sell it. Kmart did." And they base this off of a recorded statement that Eddie Fordham gave two weeks later. Now Eddie Fordham talked with Officer O'Neal for thirty minutes before his recorded statement, and then he gave a seventeen-page recorded statement in which there is one segment that says, "We went to Kmart because we had to get some ammunition. So we went there and got some ammunition. Uh, they didn't have any there, so we then went to Wal-Mart on Highway 29 to buy more." And based on that, Wal-Mart says, they purchased the ammunition at Kmart. Ladies and gentlemen, what does Officer O'Neal say? Officer O'Neal says, "I am the one who took the statement. It was absolutely clear and specific that Eddie was saying the ammunition came from Wal-Mart."

No one has testified that the ammunition came from Kmart. If it came from Kmart, you know Wal-Mart would have produced a cash register receipt from Kmart showing the sale of the ammunition. Moreover, why would someone go to Kmart and buy ammunition, and then immediately go to Wal-Mart and buy more ammunition? Wal-Mart is the entity that sold the ammunition used to kill Wayne Coker.

The next issue is whether Wal-Mart had reasonable cause to believe that Eddie and Patrick Bonifay were under twenty-one years of age when they purchased the ammunition. Wal-Mart says. "We didn't sell it. But if we did sell it, the boys must have had a fake ID or used an adult, and that is why we didn't have reasonable cause to believe the boys were under twenty-one." What is the evidence? Again, every single person has testified there was no fake ID and no adult was used to purchase the ammunition. Eddie Fordham was arrested two weeks after this murder, gave a recorded statement, and said he bought the ammunition. In a murder investigation, when you're picked up, the one thing you don't admit to is you bought the ammunition unless it is true. Three boys were arrested, Barth, Bonifay, and Fordham, and they are singing like canaries, is what Trooper O'Neal said. They're ratting out and telling on everybody. And not at any time has anyone ever mentioned that anyone bought the ammunition other than Fordham and Bonifay.

What else do we know? Patterson testified that the boys gave a statement. They testified at trial. There were four criminal trials. There have been all the subsequent civil depositions. Two boys have been sitting on death row for the past five years, and two have been serving a life sentence for the past five years. One thing you can count on is that if anyone else had been involved in the purchase of the ammunition, then by now someone would have said something.

What else do we know? O'Neal, the investigating officer, said there was absolutely no evidence of anyone else being involved in this purchase other than Eddie Fordham and Pat Bonifay. What does Patterson say? No evidence of anyone else being involved except Eddie Fordham and Pat Bonifay. And interestingly enough, who split the money? Eddie Fordham, Pat Bonifay, and Chris Barth, no other people. If someone else had been involved in the purchase, wouldn't they have got some money?

Let's talk about a fake ID. What do we know about that? Again, it has been five years, two people on death row, two life imprisonments. There has been an incredible amount of testimony in this case, depositions, trials, recorded statements, and yet never, ever, has anyone ever suggested a fake ID. What did Trooper O'Neal say? He said, I arrested the boys and all their belongings were checked, including ID, and there was no fake ID found, none. What did Patterson say? He said, I've prosecuted all the boys, and there was never any evidence or suggestion of a fake ID.

One thing you can count on is, after five years of this, somebody would have said something. And more importantly, Wal-Mart would have presented somebody, a parent of the boys, a girlfriend, an enemy, a friend, a neighbor, somebody would have taken the stand and said, I think they had a fake ID. There was no need for a fake ID because the boys thought they were old enough to purchase the ammunition. They thought you only had to be eighteen years of age. In fact, we know Bonifay didn't have a fake ID, because if Bonifay had had a fake ID, then why would he have had to ask Eddie Fordham, who was eighteen, to go buy ammunition for him?

So that gets us to the second part of the questions, and that is: Was Wal-Mart's sale of the ammunition a legal cause of the death of Billy Wayne Coker?

What is legal cause? Negligence is a legal cause of loss, injury, or damage if it directly and in natural and continuous sequence produces or contributes substantially to producing such loss, injury or damage so that it can reasonably be said that but for the negligence, the loss, injury, damage would not have occurred. It's the simplest test of all times. But for the negligence, violating the law, the death would not have occurred.

What do we know? The boys did not have any ammunition on Saturday night. That's why they had to go up to Kmart, but Kmart did not have any .32 ammunition. They then went to the Wal-Mart and purchased a box of .32 ammunition and loaded the gun and within three hours had shot and killed Wayne Coker. What is undisputed? Four bullets were removed from Wayne Coker's body. All four were .32 auto pistol ammunition.

The question is: Could the boys have got ammo from somewhere else within three hours? The issue is not whether these boys one day, someday, could have killed Dan Wells or one day, someday could have

161

killed someone else. The question is whether Mr. Coker would be alive. That's the issue. Mr. Coker was filling in for a sick employee. He didn't work at that store. He would not have been there any other night, according to his supervisor. If the boys couldn't get the ammunition within three hours of the time Wal-Mart sold it to them, then Trout Auto Parts would have been closed, and Wayne Coker would still be alive today.

What do we know? If these boys could have gotten ammunition from anywhere else, of course, they would have done it. You wouldn't wait until nine o'clock at night when you're about to do a robbery at midnight, to wait till the last second, go up to Kmart, not have enough money, have to go borrow money, and then go up to Wal-Mart to get it. This just would not make sense. It is clear that the boys had no other means to get the ammunition that night other than from Wal-Mart.

In answer to the first question, was there negligence, did they violate federal law, and was it a legal cause? Answer yes. What does that do? That gets you to the second question, the third question and the fourth question and the fifth question and the sixth question, and it's all the same. Was Bonifay at fault and was Eddie Fordham at fault and was Barth at fault and was Bland at fault and was Archer at fault in causing the death?

That's where we get to what's called apportionment of damages or apportionment of fault among the participants. Under the law, there's not just one legal cause. There can be a lot of people or companies that caused Mr. Coker's death.

What did it take to kill Billy Wayne Coker? It took three things. It took a gun, it took ammunition, and it took someone willing to pull that trigger. Bland had the gun, Wal-Mart had the ammunition, and Bonifay had the finger.

Let's look at those three. There is absolutely no evidence that Bland knew there was going to be any murder, and there's no evidence of any violation of the law for him giving the gun to Bonifay.

In regard to Patrick Bonifay, he is the person who murdered Wayne Coker, and he should be the most responsible.

Wal-Mart, they had over 1,500 stores in January of 1991 selling ammunition. They possibly were the largest seller of ammunition in the country at the time. What are they doing to train their employees? An employee can be twenty-one and have no background experience at all. Wal-Mart simply shows them a videotape on selling guns and ammunition, and there is literally only one sentence in the videotape addressing age, and it says you must be twenty-one for pistol, eighteen for a rifle, and if it can be used for both, you may card. That's all it says. That's Wal-Mart's whole training video. And Ken Powell, the Wal-Mart employee who sold the ammunition to Bonifay and Fordham, had not ever viewed the videotape. Moreover, the employees are not even taught which ammunition is for pistols and which ammunition is for rifles. Wal-Mart does not provide their employees a list of the ammunition telling them whether it's pistol, rifle, or interchangeable.

Ms. Lawson was the head gun and ammunition trainer for Wal-Mart, and she didn't even know that nine-millimeter was handgun ammunition. She thought it was rifle ammunition. Remember, McCaa, the owner of Gulf Breeze Pistol parlor, I specifically asked him what type of ammo is nine-millimeter, is it pistol or rifle or interchangeable? Answer, it's primarily a handgun cartridge, meaning it's primarily used in a pistol. Yet, Ms. Lawson and Ken Powell thought nine-millimeter was solely rifle ammunition and could be sold to someone eighteen years of age. Wal-Mart was the adult here. They were the ones selling ammunition at 1,500 stores. They've got to take the responsibility to better train their people.

What happened this night? Wal-Mart had a twenty-two-year-old with no experience selling ammunition working on a Saturday night with no supervisor. It was late on a Saturday night; he was about to close. He was in a hurry. He wanted to close, and he sold the ammunition out of ignorance in violation of federal law. Wal-Mart violated a federal law. What did they think was going to happen when they sold that ammunition? It was Saturday night at nine o'clock; two boys come in to buy pistol ammunition with no adult supervision. What did Wal-Mart think was about to take place?

Wal-Mart and Bonifay should be the most liable when you determine on the verdict form how to split up damages.

Let's get to the real issue, compensation. What does Wal-Mart say? Wal-Mart says that Mr. Coker was a criminal, a drug addict, an adulterer, a wife beater, a child beater, committed tax fraud, was chronically unemployed, and that he and his wife were about to get a divorce, and this family is better off without Mr. Coker.

Wal-Mart says Mr. Coker was a criminal. What is the real fact? Mr. Coker was arrested twice in his entire life, once for a bad check, and once for failure to appear because he was on the road truck driving, and yet Wal-Mart describes him as a criminal.

Wal-Mart says Mr. Coker was a drug addict. What is the real fact? There is one reference in one United Way record referencing that Ray called Sandra, and Sandra said something about drugs and alcohol. Ms. Coker admitted to everything in the world in these records, everything on the stand. If there had been any evidence of drug or alcohol, it would be in those records, and Sandra would have talked about them. Look at the autopsy. No alcohol, no drugs, and no health problems such as liver. They have all those records. And you will see it, there is nothing about drugs or alcohol. Whoever typed the United Way record typed it up wrong or misunderstood something.

Wal-Mart says Mr. Coker was an adulterer. What is the real fact? He had an affair in 1983, eight years before his death, and he came back home. But Wal-Mart says that Wayne was an adulterer.

Wal-Mart says Mr. Coker was a wife beater and a child beater. What is the real fact? Mrs. Coker admitted they had physical confrontations in 1983 when they pushed each other around. You have more medical records than imaginable. And you go through each one and you will not find in one case, not one sentence, not anything that says anything about beating or hitting or anything. Mrs. Coker used the term "abusive." And what does that mean? She meant he was screaming at the children. He would yell. He would spank them to discipline them. If there had been any evidence of abuse of these children, don't you think there would be some record somewhere, whether a police record or medical record? Look at all these cards and letters between these kids and their father and the love with these kids and what the co-employees said about Wayne and his relationship with his children.

What is true is that Sandra Coker is ill. She has a mental anxiety disorder. Unfortunately, she has problems dealing with stress and everything gets magnified. To her, yelling is abuse. Discipline is wrong. She can't drive. She can't go on the interstate. She can't go over bridges. She can't go over overpasses. She can't go in elevators. It's an illness. And Wal-Mart is taking advantage of it to mislead you.

Wal-Mart says Mr. Coker committed tax fraud. What is the real fact? He didn't file his tax returns on time, and when he did, he got a refund. He didn't even owe any money. Plus there were W-2s, which means these employers took taxes out. Yet Wal-Mart said he committed tax fraud.

Wal-Mart says that Wayne and Sandra were about to get divorced. They cite Sandra's psychological records for this. What is the real fact? This family had been through a lot of hardship. They had been homeless and without food. They had been without shelter. They had been without employment. Wayne was dealing with Sandra's illness. His son Christopher is hyperactive, has to be on Ritalin. He's bouncing off walls. He has an IQ less than 80. Wayne Coker had lived with this for eight years—more than eight years. There wasn't going to be a divorce. Sandra never spoke with an attorney. She never looked at papers. This was simply Sandra's way of venting frustration.

Wal-Mart says Mr. Coker was chronically unemployed and poor. That was the theme of Wal-Mart's case. What is the real fact? These people are poor. This man was going from job to job to job trying to get a better job for his family. He had been working at Trout for a year doing overtime, full-time. And yes, they're poor. They were making only $10,000.00 a year, but he was doing his best. Sandra can't work. Wayne was doing his best to provide for his kids, his children.

The first question in regard to compensation is going to be the amount of support for Sandra Faye Coker, the loss of support and services because of his death, the loss of support and services for Christopher, and the loss of support and services for Michelle.

What does that mean? Mr. Coker was earning $10,000.00 a year. What was being done with that money? It was paying rent, utilities, clothing, and food. Yes, he couldn't make ends meet, but that is what the $10,000.00 was going to. And they don't have that now, and, therefore, they have sustained a financial loss of $10,000 per year.

What about support and services? Services, what are they referring to? Transportation. Going grocery shopping. Helping around the house. Taking them to doctors' appointments. Everything that he was doing for that family you have to evaluate. They now are having to take cabs. They can't travel. They can't get out of the house. They can't go places. What is the value of this loss. If the figure is $20,000, then you take $20,000 and you multiply it times five, because it has been five years since Wayne's death. That means twenty times five is $100,000, and then you split that between Sandra, Michelle, and Christopher in their respective places, and you put $33,000.00 for each for the past.

Let's talk about the future. You then do the same for the future until Christopher is twenty-five and Michelle is twenty-five. And if you say it's something like $7,500 each, then you take $7,500 until Christopher will be twenty-five, which will be nine years, and $7,500 for Michelle until she is twenty-five, which is eleven years, and then you multiply that, and you put that in the future value.

As to Sandra Coker, you need to figure out for the rest of her life, which is thirty-seven years. You've got to consider what Wayne was going to be doing for rent, utilities, clothing, transportation; what he was going to be providing her when she gets elderly and needs assistance and everything else; and you put a monetary figure on that, and that's what you put in the future. For example, if you come to the conclusion that it's $10,000 a year for Sandra Coker, then it's $360,000 in the future. If you make a determination that it's twenty, it's $720,000.

The next issue will be mental pain and suffering and loss of enjoyment of life for Christopher, Michelle, and Sandra for the rest of their lives. What have they lost?

Sandra is not going to find someone else. She's forty-eight years old. She has a mental illness. She has a hyperactive son. She can't drive. She can't work. She can't go over interstates or overpasses. She's going to be alone.

What about the kids? What's reality for Christopher? Christopher has an IQ of less than 80. He's hyperactive. He's on Ritalin. What do you think his chances are of going from job to job? What are his chances for a family, making it work and not leaving?

Michelle, what about the obstacles she has to face in marriage and raising children and employment and financial times?

I would like you to consider the following when thinking about these damages. Mr. Coker met a woman for one month and married her. Over the next eleven years he had to deal with her illness, deal with his son's hyperactivity, deal with losing his job at the police force because of marital problems. He was homeless, and without food and clothes. He was living out of cars with his family. Yet this man never walked away or gave up on his family. How easy it would have been for him to wake up and say, "it's over, bye, I'm gone," and moved back to Jackson, Mississippi, found himself a job making minimum wage, met someone else, and just left his family? But he never did this and he never gave up. Wayne didn't turn to drugs. He didn't turn to crime. Wayne Coker had a tremendous gift. He understood the loyalty of family and understood the importance of not giving up even when life is very cruel and tough. He continued to try to assist his family and give them a better life, despite his enormous weaknesses. Sandra, Christopher, and Michelle will never find such a loyal and understanding individual as Wayne Coker, a person who stood by them no matter what.

When you are completing your verdict form, do not make any reductions. You figure out what the total loss is, and you figure out what Wal-Mart and all others are responsible for, and the judge will make the appropriate reductions to determine who pays what. Also, any benefits or assistance the Coker family may be getting, you do not consider that. That, again, is something the judge will take care of and make the appropriate reductions. You provide the entire loss and somebody else takes care of the reductions.

We have the burden of proof. It is the greater weight of the evidence. We do not have to prove anything beyond a reasonable doubt. That's a criminal case. No one is going to jail in this case as a result of your verdict. I like to look at burden of proof like a scale of justice. Who put on the most persuasive evidence? If the scale tips in our favor, then we win. There's going to be unanswered questions. There's going to be possibilities. There will be doubt. There's going to be speculation. That's not what is the law. Determine what is the more likely scenario, and that's who wins. A case is like a jigsaw puzzle. Once you get enough pieces, you know what the puzzle is. We can't sit here and put on every piece of the puzzle. We would be here for weeks and months and years. Mr. Gill and I have lived with this case for many years. We know more about this case than anyone else could possibly know. If there was any evidence that would have been beneficial to either side, you would have seen it. Don't go back and start thinking, well, we didn't see this or I don't know this or start saying, well, I know about this. Rely upon the evidence because things that you may think or may know or may have heard may be wrong, and we don't have a chance to discuss that. We don't have a chance to argue it. We don't have a chance to go back to our files and say, look, we've got something on that. We just can't do that.

Finally, I would like to talk about jury responsibility. The scale of justice is always blindfolded, and it's blindfolded because juries are not supposed to allow their personal beliefs or feelings to get in the way of a decision. Juries have to be superhuman beings to put all this aside and decide what the evidence was. One thing you can't consider is what's going to happen to this compensation. Don't go back there and start saying, I just can't give them the amount of money that I think they've really lost because I'm afraid what's going to happen. I'm afraid that maybe the children's money, after it gets out of guardianship, may be blown. I'm afraid Mrs. Coker may blow it. It's not a consideration. Moreover, what if the jury is wrong? What if the Cokers would have done the right thing and got a trust? Figure out what the loss is and hope for the best. Thank You.

## Appendix 2
## WRONGFUL DEATH OF A CHILD—$5,000,000 JURY VERDICT

### *Issue Addressed*

- Calculating damages for the wrongful death of a child

### IN THE CIRCUIT COURT IN AND FOR ESCAMBIA COUNTY, FLORIDA

Jerry and Rae Noonan, as
Personal representatives of the
Estate of Greg Noonan,
    Plaintiff,
vs.
Pensacola Aeromotive, INC.,
    Defendant.

---

### *Summary of Case*

Greg Noonan, at twenty-three years of age, was killed in a private airplane crash. The defendant admitted liability, and the sole issue at trial was the amount of compensation to be awarded the parents for the loss of their son. Pursuant to Florida law, parents are permitted to assert a claim for the loss of a child under twenty-five years of age.

The trial started at 1:15 P.M. on Monday, May, 22, 1989, and the jury began deliberations at 4:30 P.M. the same day. Five minutes after the jury started its deliberations, the jurors returned to the courtroom asking if they could award more money than the plaintiff's attorney had requested. After being told that they had the right to do whatever they desired, the jury continued deliberations, and two minutes later returned a verdict for $5,000,000, the exact amount the authors had requested.

### *Opening Statement*

May it please the Court, counsel, and you, the ladies and gentlemen of this jury. What we lawyers are getting ready to do now is make our opening statement. It's here that we tell you what we expect the evidence in the case is going to be, and it's here we tell you what we expect the judge is going to tell you the law is. But it's not evidence, and it's not law. It's lawyer talk. The evidence will come from the witness stand. The law will come to you at the end of the case when His Honor, the judge, instructs you.

As we told you when we selected the jury, this case is going to involve the life and death of the young man whose picture is placed on this board. The picture was taken while he was at Texas A&M, shortly before his graduation. He died December 14, 1985, in a plane crash when he was twenty-three years old. You will not hear about how the accident happened. About a week to ten days ago, Pensacola Aeromotive admitted they were absolutely responsible for Greg Noonan's death. They admit that, through no fault of Greg's, he died on Saturday afternoon, December 14, at 5:30 P.M., at the Pensacola Municipal Airport.

This case is going to involve who Greg Noonan was. As you look at this picture, I think it probably reflects as much about Greg as the evidence is going to reflect. Greg was a loving young man. He was tender. He was considerate. He was compassionate. He was hardworking. He was ambitious. And he was extremely patriotic. I think you can see all this in his face.

There is only one issue in this case, and you will decide that later this afternoon. The issue is what is the total amount of damages that will ever be awarded for the loss of Greg Noonan? Specifically, you must evaluate the pain and suffering that Jerry and Rae have experienced and will experience until the day of their deaths over the loss of their only son.

You will hear how Jerry and Rae Noonan, the father and mother of Greg, were both in the military. They got married, and Rae decided to get out of the military to raise a family. Jerry and Rae tried, and tried, and tried, to have a family, but found out that they could not have natural children. And they then adopted Greg, and two years later adopted Melony. Greg and Melony were not natural brother and sister, and they were not the natural children of Jerry and Rae. However, under Florida law, you are to judge the damages in this case as if Greg was the natural child of Jerry and Rae. In fact, Greg was Jerry and Rae's chosen child.

You are going to hear how Jerry and Rae Noonan raised their children. Jerry and Rae never left their children alone at home as they were growing up, even for one night. Similarly, Jerry and Rae did not want their children having to move to various schools throughout the country, and so Jerry retired from the military so that Greg and Melony could attend one school.

Greg ended up graduating number two in his high school class and received a scholarship to Texas A&M, where he thrived academically and socially. Greg was not only on his way to a promising career, but more important, as a young adult he continued to have a close bond with his parents and sister. Everything about this family was togetherness. Everything they did was as a family. And there is no way I can put this into words, but you will hear it, and you will see it.

You must evaluate the damages in this case through the eyes of the parents, and you'll see that in the verdict form there is a separate space for the father, and there is a separate space for the mother. What have they felt as to their loss? What is their suffering? What is their hurt from the day they first heard of Greg's death to the day they die?

Many times a case like this is tried on sympathy, and Pensacola Aeromotive spent a lot of time when we were picking the jury telling you that we were going to seek a sympathy verdict. I am here to tell you that we're not entitled to a sympathy verdict, we are not going to ask for a sympathy verdict, and we do not want a sympathy verdict. I think you'll realize this after you have the opportunity to meet the Noonan family and why we're going to try this case as unemotionally as possible, totally on the evidence and the law.

We do not want a sympathy verdict. A sympathy verdict is like charity. You give the plaintiff something. This is not charity. The Noonans are entitled to recover fair compensation for their loss. A sympathy case is the kind of case where you never mention an amount of money to the jury until the very end of the case. You simply put on witness after witness after witness. Ministers and relatives and friends and neighbors, and then finally at the end, you give a figure once the jury is involved in the case and feels the emotion. That is not what we are going to do, and I have decided to tell you right up front that we believe the damages in this case are five million dollars for the death of Greg. And at the end of the case, we're going to look you in the eye and tell you we believe we have proved this and ask you to award this sum.

I am getting ready to sit down. In many cases, in fact, a great majority of cases, who the lawyer is can make a lot of difference. In this case, that's not the situation. A good lawyer in this case would let the case try itself, and I hope I'm a good enough lawyer to realize that. You're not going to hear hours of argument, and days of testimony. I am getting ready to sit down. We're going to start presenting the evidence, and all the evidence will be presented within two to three hours, and we will then present the closing argument, and His Honor will instruct you on the law. At the end of the case, I am going to stand here and tell you that we believe the evidence proved what a wonderful family this was, what a wonderful young man this was, what a tremendous and painful loss this has been and always will be for Jerry and Rae, and that this case is legitimately worth five million dollars.

Thank you.

### Closing Argument

May it please the Court, counsel, and you, the ladies and gentlemen of the jury. What we're getting ready to do now is make our closing arguments in this case. I rather consider it a summation, not an argument, because I don't think there is much to argue about. It's here that we give you our impression of the evidence. It's here we give you our thoughts about what the judge is going to tell you the law is. But again, what we say is not evidence. It's not law. It's lawyer talk. The evidence came from the witness stand. And the law is going to come to you in a very few minutes from His Honor.

I would be remiss if I didn't thank you for your patience and attention. I realize it was a short trial. It was intentionally a short trial. I did not want it to become an emotional, sympathetic type of case. As to your patience and attention, I'm not only thanking you for my clients, but also for His Honor, as well as for Mr. Helmsing and his client, Pensacola Aeromotive Corporation.

I told you at the start that no matter how much we tried to keep sympathy out, your natural emotion when you looked at Greg's pictures and heard the testimony would be to feel sympathy. But we're not entitled to a sympathy verdict; we're not asking for a sympathy verdict, and we do not want a sympathy verdict. You say why? Well, sympathy is like charity. Sympathy would be for you to go into that jury room and to say let's give these people something. And that's not what the law provides.

In this case, I believe the evidence, the law, and logic all point to the fact that this is a five-million-dollar lawsuit. And the burden of proving this is upon us. We must prove our case to you by the evidence, by the greater weight of the evidence. Greater weight means 51%. I like to look at it like the scales of justice. On one side of the scale is our evidence, on the other side is their evidence. Which evidence weighs more? We do not have to prove anything beyond a reasonable doubt. Beyond a reasonable doubt is the test in a criminal case. In a criminal case, you must prove your case beyond and to the exclusion of every reasonable doubt. That's not the test here because this is not a criminal case; and no matter what you do, no matter how much you find in your verdict for damages in this case, nobody is going to go to jail. Nobody is going to lose his job, and nobody is going to receive a fine.

Pensacola Aeromotive says we only put on two hours of testimony. We did not bring on enough evidence of Jerry's and Rae's loss or the type of person Greg was. Well, if there was anything about the testimony that you heard that was not true, rest assured Pensacola Aeromotive would have brought evidence in. Pensacola Aeromotive is not precluded from investigating the family or investigating Greg or investigating his grades or anything else. They have access to all of this through discovery and investigators. If there was anything not true about what was said, they had a right to bring in the evidence.

Now, what are your responsibilities? When we get through with our closing arguments, and we will not be very long, you are going to be handed a verdict form. There are two spaces on the verdict form. The first paragraph of the verdict form says that Pensacola Aeromotive is 100% liable for Greg's death and the damages you award. The second paragraph asks you to fill in the past and future mental pain and suffering for Rae Noonan over the loss of her son. The third paragraph asks you to fill in the past and future mental pain and suffering for Jerry Noonan over the loss of his son.

When evaluating Jerry's and Rae's loss, there is no exact standard or measurement for how you are to place a monetary figure on this loss. However, you must evaluate the damages in this case through the eyes of the parents, through the eyes of Jerry Noonan and Rae Noonan, father and mother. And that's the reason the verdict form specifically mentions their names.

Now, how is this done? Well, it's done by evaluating the mental pain and suffering from the moment Jerry and Rae learned of their son's death to the moment they die, and you do this for Rae, and you do this for Jerry. As I said, you evaluate this through the eyes of the parents. And that's the reason we presented you evidence as to the kind of person Greg Noonan was, and we also presented evidence as to the kind of people Jerry and Rae Noonan are.

And now that you have met the Noonans and you have heard the evidence, I think that you know what I meant when I stated that this family evidences many of the good things that there are in this country, the family unit. I think that the manner in which they raised Greg was a wonderful situation. Rae quit work to have a family. She spent her whole life raising her two children. She then went back to work to help put them through college.

Jerry's and Rae's whole life was dedicated to raising the family. They have now lost their only son, a son they chose through adoption, and the son to carry on their name. And you must evaluate their loss through their eyes, their feelings, their hurt, and what they thought about their son. You must also evaluate Jerry's loss of his wife, who has never been the same since Greg's death. Even today, she has not gotten past the first stage of grief. She still believes that one day Greg will walk into the door of their home. She cannot even seek the help of a psychiatrist because she refuses to believe her son is dead.

As you look at Greg's picture up here, you can see that he was good looking, kind, loving, tender, polite, courteous, and ambitious. It is amazing that everything you can say about Greg can be seen in this one picture.

What value would be a fair amount to be awarded in this case? Your award will be 100% of everything that will ever be awarded for the loss of Greg Noonan. As I said, I submitted to you the figure of two and one-half million dollars each for a total of five million dollars. Where did I come up with it? I think you need to look around in this day and time to evaluate things. They just completed the Kentucky Derby. If the winning horse wins in the Belmont and Preakness, Chrysler Corporation is going to give the owner of the horse a five-million-dollar bonus. You think about ballplayers. The best ballplayers for a season earn two and one-half to three million. You think of pop stars, music stars, TV stars. The great pop stars receive at least five million dollars a year. You think of Madonna, who's a pop singer. She made forty-three million dollars last year. Of course, some of that money was for her posing in *Penthouse*.

What is Jerry's and Rae's loss over Greg? I certainly think their hurt and loss is more than the loss of a pop star. It is hard to imagine a better family. There is a saying that "when you lose your parents, you lose your past. When you lose your spouse, you lose your present, but when you lose a child, you lose your future." We asked you for a total of five million dollars for a lifetime. It should be more like five million dollars a year.

Mr. Helmsing will now have an opportunity to present his closing remarks, and then I will return for my final statements.

Thank you.

## Rebuttal Argument

May it please the Court, counsel, and you, the ladies and gentlemen of the jury.

I am going to just take a very few minutes in rebuttal. Mr. Helmsing, of course, is extremely eloquent. He's an excellent defense lawyer, and that is why Pensacola Aeromotive went to Mobile to get him, and you can see why. He's very, very good.

I am going to try to answer the things Mr. Helmsing pointed out. First, this case is not about punishment, and no one is going to be punished. Bill Mayo is not even a party in this case. He happens to be an officer of a corporation that used to be located at Pensacola Airport, and the corporation is the party. Bill Mayo has nothing to do with the case. We're not asking you to punish anybody. We are asking you to evaluate this case based on the facts, evidence, and law.

Mr. Helmsing says that it was wonderful Jerry and Rae didn't have their child suffer from an illness for five or six or ten months or two years. I disagree. I think if you ask any parent if he could have had ten more minutes with his child, he would always say yes. I don't think it's a fair statement to say how lucky Jerry and Rae were that their son was killed in a plane that went up into the air and all of a sudden dove back down and crashed at Pensacola Airport. I don't consider that to be a very fortunate situation as a parent.

Mr. Helmsing says money will not bring their son back. That's correct, but that is the law of Florida. You have to evaluate this in terms of money. Our system of justice no longer inflicts an eye for an eye. It doesn't happen that way anymore. We don't say, "You negligently killed my son, now I will take your son." That's not the way we do things in this country. Our system evaluates loss from a monetary standpoint. And when we evaluate things, we almost always pay more for the best. The best homes cost the most money. The best cars cost the most money. The best planes cost the most money. The best clothes, the best jewelry, everything that is better costs more. Greg was an incredible person and son, and Jerry and Rae were superb parents. They are a great representation of the family unit.

The law is that you evaluate the loss in terms of dollars. And you have the opportunity here today to do that. This is the total amount of money that will ever be awarded for the loss of this young man. Whether he would have made millions in his lifetime is not a consideration of yours. What he would have become is not your consideration. The total loss here is what you award these two parents. That is the total loss that will ever be awarded. And you have the opportunity today to decide the true values in life—the values of family and the values of a great child.

I made a commitment to you. I said that I felt like I could prove to you that two and one-half million dollars each would be a fair amount for their loss. And you know, there is no exact measurement. There is no yardstick. Mr. Helmsing is correct. There is no way you can, when you talk about a sentimental loss, go in and buy and sell these things. There is no way you can go to find the price of this loss.

I thought about a way, however. I thought about if I owned something that was sentimental, such as a baby crib that had been handed down from generation to generation to generation. And then I wanted to take this baby crib and give it to my daughter or my grandchild, and I sent it by way of Mr. Helmsing's clients, and they accidentally lost it. If we came in today, Mr. Helmsing would say his client can go get a new baby crib for $50. Yes, but the crib his client lost was handed down from my great-great-great-grandparents all the way down. It is an emotional loss, a sentimental loss. How would you go about determining the true value of my loss? The question is how much would I be willing to pay for someone to find and return the crib. For

179

example, if I had put an ad in the paper offering a reward of $10,000 for the crib, then you know the value of the crib to me is $10,000.

Thus, the question is: How much would Jerry and Rae be willing to pay or give up to have Greg back? If you believe without question that Jerry and Rae would give five million dollars to have their son back, then that would be a fair value. But you know Jerry and Rae don't have that kind of money; they don't have anywhere near five million dollars. However, do they have anything of value that they would give up to have their son back? If they had something each worth two and one-half million dollars, would they give it up? If you sincerely believe they would give it up to have Greg back, then you know how to value their loss.

I want you to assume that on December 14, 1985, Greg Noonan didn't get on that plane, but Jerry and Rae were in the plane. Jerry and Rae didn't die in the crash. I want you to assume that each of them lost both of their legs, and we were here today evaluating the loss of their legs. I don't think there would be any question in your mind that two and one-half million dollars would be peanuts for the loss of both legs. Would Mr. and Mrs. Noonan give up both of their legs and go through life in a wheelchair to have their 23-year-old son walk through these courtroom doors? If you believe they would, then I submit to you the case is worth two and one-half million dollars to each because the test for the value of something that can't be measured, some emotional loss, some sentimental loss is what would the person who lost it—not what Mr. Helmsing says, not what I say—what would *they* give up? And I submit to you that there is no question they would give up their legs to have their son back. They gave up their life for those children to begin with. They never left the kids alone at the home.

Tomorrow you will be back at work or at home, and you will have your own problems to address. In the future you will not be thinking about this case or about the Noonans unless someone ever asks you,

"Did you ever serve on a jury?" "Yes. I served on a jury. I evaluated the loss of a wonderful young man." If that doesn't come up, you'll really never think about this. You've got your own problems to think about and worry about.

Next week Mr. Helmsing will be back in court. I'll be back in court. The judge will be back in court with other cases to handle and other cases to try.

There is only one group of people who will live with your decision for the rest of their lives. And that is the Noonan family. And I say to you that you are the conscience of this community. You are the conscience of this country. And I submit that you have an opportunity to evaluate the true values in life—family. It's not the sport stars, movie stars, and pop stars.

I thank you.

## Appendix 3
## BRAIN INJURY CASE—$22 MILLION JURY VERDICT

### *Issues Addressed*

- Evaluating loss of enjoyment of life when the victim does not understand what has been lost

- Evaluating a parent's loss of consortium of their child

### IN THE CIRCUIT COURT OF THE FIRST JUDICIAL CIRCUIT, IN AND FOR WALTON COUNTY, FLORIDA

ROBERT A. CAMPBELL and
JANET CAMPBELL, individually,
and ROBERT CAMPBELL, as
legal guardian of LANA CAMPBELL,
    Plaintiffs,
v.                       Case No. 90-0891-CA
PHILLIP TURNER,
    Defendant.

---

### *Summary of Case*

On May 18, 1990, Phillip Turner ran a stop sign at an intersection in Walton County, Florida, and collided with a railroad embankment. As a result, Lana Campbell, a passenger in the vehicle, sustained catastrophic injuries.

Lana, who was seventeen years of age at the time of the collision, was taken to Humana Hospital in Fort Walton Beach, Florida, where she remained in a coma for five months. Lana's mother, Janet

Campbell, remained at the hospital during this five-month period, uncertain whether her daughter was going to live.

After five months in the hospital, Lana was able to blink her eyes and move her fingers. She was then taken to New Orleans, Louisiana, to the New Medico Rehabilitation Institute, where Lana remained until January of 1991. It was at this time that Lana's medical insurance carrier discontinued payment of Lana's medical care, and Lana was sent home. At the time Lana returned to her home, she could not speak, could not walk, had no control over her bowels or bladder, could not eat and was in a fetal position. Lana's parents, Robert and Janet, were having to physically lift Lana to move her, were having to clean her for bowel and bladder problems, were having to care for her monthly female sanitary needs, were having to feed Lana through the use of tubes, and were having to care for Lana's severe diabetes, which required the use of insulin three times per day.

Approximately three weeks after Lana returned home, she was accepted in the Capital Rehabilitation program in Tallahassee, Florida, and the medical insurance carrier approved payment. Lana's father, Robert, who was just starting his own business, took off from work every Tuesday, Thursday, and weekend to drive from DeFuniak Springs to Tallahassee so that he could be with and care for his daughter.

Five months after Lana entered Capital Rehabilitation, the facility concluded that Lana had reached maximum medical improvement, and there was nothing further that could be done for her. The medical insurance carrier therefore again discontinued medical payments, and Lana was sent home to live with her parents. When Lana returned home, she could not walk, talk, eat, or control her bowels or bladder and was in a fetal position.

Robert and Janet were again faced with having to physically lift their adult child in order to move her from her bed to the bathroom, were having to clean her for bowel and bladder problems, were having to care for her monthly female sanitary needs, were having to feed her through the use of tubes and were having to care for her diabetes.

Within four months of being at home under her parent's care, Lana began showing some signs of improvement. She began to speak in single words and began eating some food. However, she remained in a fetal position, had severe difficulty in swallowing, had a tube in her stomach for feeding, could not propel her wheelchair, was unable to dress herself or bathe herself, and was incontinent of bladder.

Janet and Robert continued to work with Lana, and over a several-year period and contrary to what the medical providers predicted, Lana made remarkable progress. In fact, as of the time of trial, Lana could speak, eat with assistance, could assist with her bathing, clothing, and some household functions. She had control over her bowels and bladder, and could walk with a cane for short distances as long as she had the assistance of an adult by her side.

Lana, however, still required twenty-four-hour supervision, as her brain function was severely impaired. She required assistance getting on and off a toilet, and with her monthly cycle. She could not prepare her meals nor care for her diabetes. She could not check her blood sugar and did not know when or how much medication to take. She did not know what type of food to eat to maintain her diabetes. She had visual problems and her physical condition was such that she could only walk with assistance and only for short distances.

At the trial, which was heavily contested by defense counsel hired by Nationwide Insurance Company, there were several forms of damages the Plaintiffs were entitled to recover: (1) Lana Campbell's past and future medical expenses; (2) Lana Campbell's past and future loss of earning capacity; (3) Lana Campbell's past and future pain and suffering, disability, physical impairment, disfigurement, mental anguish, inconvenience, and loss of capacity for the enjoyment of life; (4) Janet Campbell's past and future loss of Lana Campbell's companionship, society, love, and affection; and (5) Robert Campbell's past and future loss of Lana Campbell's companionship, society, love, and affection.

Based on the evidence presented at trial and the instructions provided by the court, the jury returned the following verdict: (1) $531,846 in past medical expenses; (2) $5,000,000 in future medical expenses; (3) $611,000 for Lana Campbell's future loss of earning capacity; (4) $2,000,000 for Lana Campbell's past pain and suffering, disability, physical impairment, disfigurement, mental anguish, inconvenience, and loss of capacity for the enjoyment of life; (5) $6,000,000 for Lana Campbell's future pain and suffering, disability, physical impairment, disfigurement, mental anguish, inconvenience, and loss of capacity for the enjoyment of life; (6) $2,000,000 for Robert Campbell's past loss of Lana Campbell's companionship, society, love, and affection; (7) $2,000,000 for Robert Campbell's future loss of Lana Campbell's companionship, society, love, and affection; (8) $2,000,000 for Janet Campbell's past loss of Lana Campbell's companionship, society, love, and affection; and (9) $2,000,000 for Janet Campbell's future loss of Lana Campbell's companionship, society, love, and affection.

After the jury trial, we proceeded with the bad-faith trial against Nationwide Insurance Company to collect the excess judgment. We were successful at trial, and the jury concluded that Nationwide had acted in bad faith in not getting the case settled within days after the accident. The trial judge, however, granted a judgment for the defense notwithstanding the verdict. We appealed, but lost the issue on appeal. The family's recovery was limited to $110,000.

The closing argument presented appears below:

*Closing Argument*

May it please the court, counsel, and you, the ladies and gentlemen of this jury. On May 18, 1990, as a result of Mr. Turner's conduct and through no fault of Lana's, Lana was placed in a coma. She was taken to Humana Hospital where she remained for five months. At her side at all times was her mother. Lana could not speak, could not walk, had no control of her bowels and bladder, had tubes to feed her, and no one knew if she was going to live or die. After five months of Janet by her side and not being able to work and not knowing the future of her daughter, the hospital finally saw a glimmer of hope when they spoke with Lana, and she could blink her eyes and move her fingers. To them that was good enough that Lana was ready for rehab in New Orleans, and they sent her to New Orleans, and Janet followed her, and Janet was by her side until November when her son came down with diabetes, and she had to go home, and then Robert started filling in.

Lana was in New Medico facility in New Orleans until January of '91, approximately seven months after this incident. She still could not speak, she could not walk, she had no control of her bowels or bladder, she could not eat, she was being fed from a tube, she was basically a vegetable. But because there was no progress, Mailhandlers Insurance said. "We are not paying anymore; that is it," and sent her home. Janet and Robert begged, "You can't do this. How can we possibly care for Lana?" The insurance company says, "That is not our problem."

Lana came home for three weeks in January. She was in a fetal position, she had tubes in her body, she could not eat, she could not walk, she had no control of her bowels and bladder, she could not speak, and she could not respond. Robert and Janet were having to physically lift their child of eighteen years of age, they were having to clean their eighteen-year-old child, they were having to take care of her monthly sanitary needs, and they were having to feed their daughter through a tube. Approximately three weeks later, after begging and crying, they were finally able to get their daughter to Tallahassee into a rehab center. They took her into a rehab unit in Tallahassee, and Robert, who was trying to start a new business, took off every Tuesday and Thursday to drive to Tallahassee to help rehab his daughter; his daughter who cannot speak, who cannot communicate, who cannot walk. The family drives over every weekend. Close to a year after this collision Tallahassee rehab gives up. They turn to Robert and Janet and say that the only thing the doctors can agree on is that your daughter will never walk, talk, eat, have any control of her bowels, and you have got to take her home.

Their daughter came home, and for the first time since their child was an infant they were faced with a 24-hour job; to pick their daughter up to take her to the bathroom, to feed her, to try to get her to talk, to try to open her jaws, to try to rehab her legs. They spent all their waking time with her, and within four months Lana could speak, she had control over her bowels, she had partial control of her bladder, she could eat some foods, and she was beginning to live. For the next three years their lives consisted of getting up at 4:30 or 5:00 in the morning to make sure their daughter was okay, to make sure her diabetes was under control, to make sure she had not gone to the bathroom on herself, to make sure her bowels and bladder were functioning, to make sure she was being fed, to carry her where she needed to go, to lift her head when it was pulling to the side, to go to work all day, and to come home to begin again.

It's now seven and a half years later. What Janet and Robert have accomplished according to Dr. Vervoort is remarkable. No one ever thought it was possible. Lana is a gorgeous child. She sits up here as innocent as innocent can be. She can remember her second-grade teacher, and she can do division and simple math, but she can't remember that her sister lives with her right now; she can't remember what month it is or when Christmas is. She can't remember what she had for breakfast. She has no ability to care for herself, no judgment. She is at the whim of the world around her. She has no way to protect herself from evil people. If she is in a facility, she has no way to distinguish whether someone is doing something good or something bad. What is that person's motive, what is their background, what is he going to do to Lana now or in the next sixty years? Who is it that is working with Lana in that facility and what are his real motives? Lana has no way to distinguish that or protect herself and never will. That is why we are here today.

This is not TV, this is reality. You seven people will make a decision today that will decide this family's future. There is no coming back; there is no second trial; there is no second attempt. You today will make the sole decision that will control Lana's sixty years of life from this point forward. There is no coming back. You will decide whether Lana gets professional residential care for the rest of her life with people who you know what their training is, people you know what their motives are, people that you control in your household, people that you watch every day, people that when they don't do the right thing you get rid of them, people that you have control over as parents and grandparents. You get to decide whether that is what Lana gets or whether Lana is going to be at the whim of HRS, and what they decide to do in the future, what they decide to cut back or give more, at the whim of whether Mailhandlers decides she needs rehab or not, whether Janet will work for the rest of her life to keep Mailhandlers. Whether Janet and Robert will beg and cry for the rest of their lives for government facilities, Medicaid facilities, and insurance.

What is enjoyment of life? It's different for everybody. It can be sharing time with your spouse, sharing time with your children or grandchildren, being in the church, playing sports, enjoying nature, enjoying a book. Enjoyment of life changes for everybody during time. What you will enjoy at twenty is not what you will enjoy at sixty. What enjoyment of life comes down to is freedom. It's freedom to live where you want, be with who you want, go where you want, do what you want, and the freedom to change along the way. Lana Campbell will never have that freedom. She'll never have those choices. Never. She'll be where her parents have the ability to take care of her, and after her parents are gone who knows? Lana Campbell will never have the joy of falling in love and getting married and walking down an aisle and giving birth, never have the joy of having her child crawl for the first time, speak for the first time, say the crazy things kids say, go off to schools for the first time and come home and want to talk about everything. She will never have the pleasure of watching her child go off and get married and become an adult and raise grandchildren.

Lana will never have any choices. That is why there is a legal guardian to make those choices. But the loss of freedom is not only Lana's loss, it's also Robert's and Janet's loss because they have given up their freedom of choice. It's like raising a four-year-old for the rest of your life. You don't have the choice to go out anymore or go on vacation or go to a movie.

Everything you do must revolve around Lana for the rest of your life. Janet is forty-three and Robert is forty-seven. According to the Florida mortality tables, Janet has forty-two more years of life and Robert has thirty-three. For the next thirty to forty years their freedom is gone. Their lives will revolve around Lana and the care they can get for her.

In a little while you will be sent back, and you will be given a verdict form and the verdict form will be identical to this one. And the very first question is what is Lana's past medical expenses. It's unrefuted. It's $531,846. Now you heard about Mailhandlers paying some, Medicaid paying some, the government paying some, whatever. As we talked about earlier, that is not an issue. That is something the court takes care of later depending upon how much has been paid. The medicals are $531,846. You're not to consider those other issues.

The second question is future medicals. The State of Florida, Division of Head Injury, saw Lana, and they said we need to get her to a specialist, and they sent her to Dr. Shane Vervoort, the doctor that was here.

Dr. Vervoort has cared for her since that time, and what did he tell you? There are only five options for Lana. One, she can remain with her parents for the rest of her life, and she can be provided care by someone like Janet if Janet could quit her job. He says that is the ideal situation for Lana's future. That is also impossible. Janet and Robert both have to work.

Dr. Vervoort said the second option is that Lana remain at home and they get a professional person experienced with head injury, someone they know, someone they can control, someone who they know will be motivated at all times to come into the household on a ten-hour basis, seven days a week to work with Lana.

The third option he said is for Lana to be in a special facility, a residential facility, living with six people, where they have people specifically trained for head injuries, people specially trained to deal with people like Lana, and he said that costs $250 a day.

The fourth option he said is to allow Lana to continue like she is in the household and going into A.R.C. or other facilities like that.

He said the last option is to put Lana in a facility such as a rest home or a nursing home or with someone who has the capability to maintain her. He said this last option is the worst option. He said the problem is when you deal with option four, which is the A.R.C. and stuff like that, and you deal with facilities such as nursing homes or rest homes, they have limited resources. They don't have the staff to give Lana individual attention to deal with her head injury, to make sure she is walking and physically active, to stimulate her. You don't know exactly who is in that facility, you don't know who they have hired, what their background is, you don't know what their motivation is.

We say that there is only one option here and that is that Lana remains with her family and that you award the money necessary to have a professional person that they can hire come in seven days a week, ten hours a day to work with Lana. A person they can trust when Janet and Robert want to go off to a movie or go on vacation or if they just need a break.

Dr. Vervoort says that the cost will at least be $250 a day if not more. At $250 a day it's approximately ninety thousand dollars a year and over Lana's life expectancy, which is approximately sixty years according to the tables, it's over five million dollars.

The next question is what is the amount of damages for lost earning ability to be sustained by Lana Campbell in future years. This is simple. Lana cannot work and she never will work. There is no question. She requires 24-hour supervision, she has no short-term memory. She can remember long-term things sometimes such as her second grade teacher or math, but she can't remember things now. She can't be taught to remember about her medication, how much to take or when to take it. She has no way to hold employment.

If you just say she was never going to earn more than minimum wage, then that is five dollars an hour times forty hours a week at two hundred dollars a week times fifty weeks is ten thousand dollars a year. She is twenty-five. She would have worked another forty years to age sixty-five. Ten thousand dollars a year times forty years is four hundred thousand dollars.

The next question is what is the damages for Lana Campbell—what is the amount of damages Lana Campbell has experienced for pain and suffering, disability, physical impairment, disfigurement, mental anguish, inconvenience, and loss of capacity for the enjoyment of life in the past and the future. I would like to sum it up as loss of enjoyment of life. A week before this collision Lana was graduating her senior year. You have seen the pictures of how gorgeous she looks. We talked about how meticulous she was and how clean she was. How she had dreams of being a designer, how she had hopes in the future. She was looking forward to graduation; she was getting her cap and gown. She was eighteen years old, the time when you're going off to experience independence for your first time in life, the time when you're going to meet your first love for the first time, the time when you will be getting married for hopefully the first and only time, the time when you will be having children, the time when you grow a special bond between yourself and your parents that you didn't have as a child because you're on your own, and you are starting to realize what life is really about. That is what Lana has missed.

In the future Lana has fifty-nine to sixty years of life left. Sixty years is an unbelievably long time. Very few people in this courtroom today are sixty years old. Robert Campbell had not even lived fifty years. When you think about the amount of life that takes place in sixty years. Sixty years ago it was 1937. Since that time we have had World War II, Korea, Bay of Pigs, Vietnam, and the Gulf War. Our country has been led by Franklin Roosevelt, Harry Truman, Dwight Eisenhower, John F. Kennedy, Lyndon Johnson, Richard Nixon, Gerald Ford, Jimmy Carter, Ronald Reagan, and George Bush. Sixty years ago, the minimum wage was forty cents per hour. We have had the McCarthy red scare, the Kennedy assassination, the Bobby Kennedy assassination, President Reagan was shot. It was less than thirty years ago that a man set foot on the moon. Sixty years is a very long time when you think about what all Lana will miss, her freedom.

My suggestion is that when you talk about the future loss of enjoyment of Lana Campbell, you consider that, if her medical bills are five million dollars just to keep her in a safe and healthy and happy place, then the loss of enjoyment of life has to exceed that because it doesn't otherwise make sense. Our enjoyment has to exceed the amount of money we are willing to spend to stay in existence. While that sounds like an incredible sum of money, it's trivial. When you compare to what society does in order to save enjoyment of life—when somebody is in a burning building we never ask the person's age, we never ask the person's race, we never ask if it's a male or female, we don't ask if the person is rich or poor, good or bad. If a person is lost at sea, none of those questions are relevant. We will send the Coast Guard, helicopters, divers, whatever it takes to save the enjoyment of life. There is not one person who would ever, ever criticize a pilot, a military pilot for bailing out of an eight-million-dollar jet to save his own life. You would expect it.

The next and last two questions are what is the amount of any damages sustained by Robert Campbell for the loss of Lana Campbell's companionship, society, love, and affection in the past and in the future. And the next question is what is the amount of any damages sustained by Janet Campbell for the loss of Lana Campbell's companionship, society, love, and affection. Janet and Robert live for Lana. She is great, she is beautiful and she provides them tremendous joy. But they have lost something. They have lost their freedom and Lana's freedom. They have lost Lana's ability to grow and mature and develop her own life and to have children.

They have lost the ability of Lana being with them when they age. It is so unnatural in life. The natural order is for them to raise their children, and then when they get older the children will care for them. That will never occur. When Robert and Janet get older and can't care for themselves, all they are going to be able to think about is Lana and what is going to happen to her. Will she be safe? Will they forget to bring her insulin, will they leave her unattended, will they care for her as they have, will there be good people working with her, will there be bad people? Because as they get older, Lana gets older too, and as Dr. Vervoort said, it's much more difficult. Lana will not be able to move as well or think as well. To their last days no matter what happens, 24 hours they are going to be with Lana thinking about her.

The last thing I want to talk about is jury responsibility. As you can tell, I am asking for more money than anybody probably ever imagined when we walked in this courtroom. Everybody knows that Mr. Turner can never pay this money, but in voir dire each of you promised me that you would follow the law. The law doesn't ask whether Lana was injured by Ford Motor Company or Phillip Turner. The law is the Lady of Justice. We have all seen her. The Lady of Justice is blindfolded. There is a reason for that blindfold. It's because justice is not permitted to look at anything other than the facts and the law. You can't look at whether the defendant is rich or poor, old or young. You can't look at whether he never pays. When you go back there, the purpose we are here about is for you to follow the law and determine today what Lana and the Campbells have lost. That is the only issue here.

If you honestly go back there and you say it's the millions and millions and millions I am asking you for, then that is what you have got to write down. And it doesn't matter who is paying it, whether the medical insurance has been paying for it or the government or whatever. When you come back in this courtroom, your verdict is going to speak. It's going to speak about the value of loss of enjoyment of life. It's going to speak about what the Campbells have done and what they have been through. It's going to speak about what they are going to have to go through the remainder of their lives. It's going to speak about what Lana is going to go through. And I ask that your verdict speak the truth and not on any other issues.

Thank you.

## Appendix 4
## MOTOR VEHICLE ACCIDENT–WRONGFUL DEATH OF ADULT CHILD–$1 MILLION JURY VERDICT

### Issue Addressed

• Explaining a parent's mental pain and suffering over the loss of a child

## IN THE CIRCUIT COURT IN AND FOR ESCAMBIA COUNTY STATE OF FLORIDA

THE ESTATE OF PAMELA DENISE
WILLIAMS,
    Plaintiff,
vs.
NATIONAL CAR RENTAL SYSTEM, INC.
    Defendant.

---

### Summary of Case

Pamela Williams, an African-American, was killed in an automobile accident when she was riding as a passenger in a vehicle and returning home during a break at the University of Florida. The case was tried before an all-white jury in Pensacola, Florida, in 1981. Below are excerpts from the opening portion of closing argument and the rebuttal. As you can tell from reading the rebuttal, the defense attorney did not believe that an all-white jury would award significant money to a minority plaintiff, and openly attacked the parents. The jury returned a one-million-dollar jury verdict, the largest jury verdict in the state of

Florida, and possibly the country, for the death of child (black or white) as of that time.

### Excerpts of Closing Argument

May it please the Court, counsel, and you, the ladies and gentlemen of this jury. First, I want to thank you for the kind patience and attention you have shown us here today. I'm speaking not only for myself and my clients, but I'm speaking for Mr. Condon and Mr. Bridgers and their clients.

This is the closing argument and this is when we give you our impressions of the evidence, and it is here that we tell you what we expect the judge will instruct as to the law. But again, it's not evidence, it's lawyer talk. The evidence came off the witness stand, and the law will come to you from His Honor.

Today you have had the opportunity to hear the testimony about one of the most fabulous, fantastic young ladies I guess that you could ever imagine. It becomes more fabulous when you realize that she was only nineteen years old when she died. My thought was "Could it be a dream?" But, no, it's real. She was real. Her death was real. And the suffering of her parents have been real. She's now touched your lives through the testimony, and I don't believe anybody could come in contact with Pamela Williams and not feel sympathetic over her cruel and untimely death. But, as we discussed in opening statement and as I discussed when I selected you on the jury, when you step into the jury room in a few minutes, that's not a place for sympathy. You have got to judge this case on the evidence and the law.

Now, I disagree with Mr. Condon. Mr. Condon told you in opening statement, he said, "Now, if this were a sympathy verdict, then you're talking about a lot of money." No, a verdict based on the evidence and the law is when you're going to be talking about a lot of money. You see, a sympathy verdict is when you walk into the jury room and you say to yourselves, really, there is no evidence to award anything, but we want to give them something; we want to perform charity. And being the nature of charity, it's low. That's a sympathy verdict. A verdict based on the evidence and the law, as we'll discuss in a few minutes, will be very, very substantial.

Although Pam was killed in an accident, this is not a criminal case. This is a civil case for damages. Today you're going to decide all of the damages that will ever be awarded as a result of the death of Pamela Denise Williams. There are no other cases. And when you were selected on this jury you promised to follow the law and the evidence, and if that law and the evidence after you heard it required you to put in the verdict form a very, very substantial sum of money, you stated you would not be afraid to do that. You would not be afraid to do what is right.

The evidence in this case is totally uncontested. There is no testimony contrary to anything that's been put on the witness stand and every bit of it was consistent. Pam was the third of four daughters to Mr. and Mrs. James Williams. Everything Mr. and Mrs. Williams did they did for those girls. Although they loved all of them and there wasn't any question about their love for all of them, Pam was that one who had everything, and she was deservingly the apple of the eyes of James Williams and Helen Williams. Unfortunately, one of the facts that I think has become very clear to you is that Mrs. Williams began living her life through Pam, and this was an unfortunate situation. You know, as a parent, you love all of your children, some in different ways and for different reasons. In Pam's situation she just happened to be that one in a million, that dream child that had everything. You know, she was a straight person, and I use that in the best sense of the word. Because in this day and time when you're going through school and college the straights are considered to be some sort of weird. She was

197

straight, but very, very popular. She was a churchgoer. She didn't drink. She didn't smoke. She didn't curse. And when you think that this type of girl was president of her class, captain of the cheerleader's squad, she was loved by everyone. She was at the University of Florida for a little over a year. That is in Gainesville, 350 miles away from here. Yet, approximately seventy-five students, black and white, traveled a total of 700 miles to come to her funeral. To think that any one person in a year could touch that many lives and affect that many people, and that many people would have loved her is a thing of note.

Pamela loved children. This is shown by her relationship with a sister who was twelve years younger than she was—taking her to games, and taking her to parties with her. Pam volunteered to work with underprivileged children with the YWCA, and the YWCA elected her to their Board of Directors. This is not any little board, this is the big board, and Pamela was the youngest board member ever selected in the YWCA's history. She helped children through the summer Bible work that she did, including the Bible School during the last summer of her life. It was a five-day-a-week voluntary work program dealing with small children.

She respected and adored her parents. You heard the letter that was read to you and you will be able to take that into the jury room with you. She was ambitious. I think all of the testimony is consistent that Pam would have succeeded in anything that she set her mind to do. And I have no doubts that you believe from the testimony that she would have. She was bright. She had a 3.25 grade point average at the University of Florida going into her sophomore year. That's above a B average.

She was beautiful. You can see the pictures. She did community work through her efforts at the YWCA and things of that nature. She was athletic, on the varsity softball team in high school. She competed in a physical education competition in which 550 girls competed, and she was the number one physical education student. She was also very mature. One of the teachers said that when she came into that classroom it was her first year and Pam's first year, and there was all heck being raised; Pam calmed them down. Pam had control.

She was a caring person. She worked her heart out for her school. She was voted best all around in her high school class, and we could go on and on and on.

Pamela Denise Williams would have grown up to be an outstanding citizen, and I submit to you that her loss was not just a loss to Mr. and Mrs. Williams; it was a loss to our community. It was a loss to our state. And I submit to you that it may have been a loss to our nation. And I don't believe that I'm being overly optimistic when I tell you that I think there could have been great things in store for Pam Williams.

I cannot believe that anyone has ever heard any testimony about suffering any more than what you heard today from anybody's family. Three people's lives were destroyed in this accident: Pam's, Mrs. Williams', and Mr. Williams'.

You're going to be handed in this case a verdict form, and it's going to be just a little piece of paper and it's going to say: "We, the jury, find for the plaintiffs and we assess their damages as follows," and the first thing on there is going to be for the unreimbursed funeral and medical expenses, and it's already typed in: "Two Thousand, Three Dollars and Thirty-Two Cents ($2,003.32)." That's for the amount they had to come up with out of their pockets that has not been reimbursed by insurance. You'll have two other spaces. One is for James Williams. There is a dollar sign and a line. And then the next line is for Helen Williams and there is a dollar sign and a line, and that is where you as a jury are going to fill in an amount. The judge will tell you that you must award an amount of money that will adequately and fairly compensate for this tragic loss. He will go on to tell you that there are some things that you need to consider in determining this. One of the things is the loss of services that Pam would have performed for her parents, you know, the things for Tara, the cooking, the things like that. Then he will go on to tell you that there is another element of damages that doesn't stop when Pam would have become twenty-one and that is each parent's mental pain and suffering from the date of this accident for the rest of their lives.

And what does that mean? What is mental pain and anguish? You have heard an awful lot as to what these people are going through. You must attempt to look at their loss through their eyes. What do they believe they lost when they lost Pam? That's what you will be evaluating.

Now, I want to talk just a moment about Mrs. Williams and evaluate her suffering. And I told you or I asked you in opening statement to put a figure on an hour of what she goes through every day. She thinks about her daughter every minute of every hour, as you heard from all the witnesses. It never stops. She gets very little sleep. She wants to be alone. And I asked you to think of what figure you would put on an hour of that. I'm sure there are some figures probably from five dollars to fifty dollars an hour. Maybe even more than that. From the time of the accident until today it's been one and a half years, a little over that. Her life expectancy as I read to you is twenty-one and one-half years. So, we're talking about twenty-three years.

Mrs. Williams' suffering has been horrendous, and it likely will get worse. The number of hours of past and future suffering is staggering. Three hundred sixty-five days times twenty-three years is 8,395 days times twenty-four hours is 201,480 hours if she lives out her life expectancy. That is what we're talking about. For those of you who thought five dollars an hour was realistic, that's over a million dollars. For those of you who thought ten dollars an hour was realistic, it's over two million dollars. Twenty dollars an hour is over four million dollars.

Mr. Williams, according to the mortality tables, will live two years fewer than Mrs. Williams, which means he will experience a total of 183,960 hours of suffering. Mr. Williams said he wished he could work seven days a week. It would be better, because it is only during work that he gets any break from thinking about Pamela. He says the worst times are when he is at home and sees the suffering of his wife. He says he not only lost his daughter, but he also has lost his wife.

I submit to you that one million dollars should be placed in each of those verdict spaces for a total of two million dollars for the loss of Pamela Denise Williams through the eyes of her parents. It's your decision to make. Obviously, I can't make it for you. And you have a perfect right, obviously, to determine, well, maybe he's too high or maybe he's too low. You can come back with any amount that you feel is fair in this case. Probably most of you are thinking right now, "Well, he's talking within reason, the lawyer is. It sounds logical. If it was five dollars an hour, that's an awful low amount and that's really all we're talking about. Why, I might even think about going higher."

But, you haven't heard from them yet. The defense hasn't had their chance to speak. But I can predict much of what they're going to say, because I have heard the story before. They are trained. They are defense lawyers. And when they don't have the evidence and they don't have the law, they go to use slogans—slogans like "Money won't bring her back" or "What are they trying to do, profit from this?" When they get up here, make them talk about the evidence, because if they try the slogan approach, all they are trying to do is get you not to apply the evidence and the law.

The law used to be an eye for an eye. It used to be a tooth for a tooth; that is, if you took my child accidentally, then I should take your child. Then it developed to where if you accidentally took my child, then you would go to jail. Then finally there developed in this country the theory of compensation that all of you agreed on when I asked each of you specifically individually, "Do you agree that this is the fairest and the best method?" and each of you said yes. In this country you can't punish somebody for accidentally doing anything, and you can't throw him in jail for it, but you can force him to pay for this type of situation.

When Mr. Condon starts these slogans, I would like to ask you to think what is it the defense really would like? What are they really trying to do? They don't want to go back to a child for a child and to go to jail for the loss of a child. That's not the answer. What they are saying is that the defendants should walk away from this thing. They do not want you to apply the law. They do not want you to apply the evidence.

Another defense tactic's going to be, I submit to you, that Pam would have had a career. She would have married and she would have left home. But, you know, the love of a child is different from the love of a husband and wife. If a spouse leaves for two or three years, the love starts to fade. But, the love of a parent for a child, that's a different thing. It's the pride experienced when a child goes off and goes to school or goes into the service or makes a career and becomes happy. These are feelings of love and this is expected; you know, that these things will happen. And love continues until the parent's death. Had Pam lived, when it came time for Mrs. Williams to die and when it came time for Mr. Williams to die, they would have felt secure with the knowledge that Pam was happy, Pam was alive, Pam was well, and Pam was moving forward. And that's what this thing called immortality is. Immortality is the knowledge that there is that fabulous human being that will be there after you.

I suggest to you that you use your common sense when you go in that jury room and make these decisions. We have suggested to you two million dollars, and as I said, it could be too high or too low. But that figure comes out to five dollars an hour for what they go through, and that is low. And you have the power to raise it or to lower it. But, let's use our common sense for a while and think about things that go on around us every day and see, is two million dollars too much money? When you think that in this day and time great personalities—I'm talking about the great baseball and basketball players—make a million dollars a season. You think about the great fighters, the Sugar Ray Leonards and the Muhammad Alis, that make eight to ten million dollars for a fight, fifteen rounds—the most it could go is forty-five minutes—three minutes a round. You think about great movie stars, Richard Burton and these kind of people, several million dollars for a motion picture. These are the times we're living in. But here we're not talking about a season of three or four months. We're not talking about a forty-five minute fight. We're not talking about several motion pictures. Here we are talking about Mr. and Mrs. Williams' lifetime.

## Rebuttal Argument

May it please the Court, counsel, and you, the ladies and gentlemen of the jury. First, I would like to just comment about one of the things Mr. Condon said, and then I will get to the rest of it. That was, he's talked about interest on money. Now, the mere fact that if you were to award a million dollars to Mrs. Williams doesn't mean she ends up with a million dollars. But, let's say that you awarded her whatever amount it takes for her to end up with a million dollars and she invests it. A million dollars is to be invested. Assume she lives twenty-five years, and let's assume interest is at, say, an average of 10%. She would draw 10% interest on a million dollars, which would be a hundred thousand dollars per year. But, then there is a thing called Uncle Sam who comes in and takes an unearned income interest tax rate of 70%, so she ends up with thirty thousand. So, then she has a million and thirty thousand dollars for next year. But what about inflation? She's got less next year than she had this year, and for that reason, the Court is going to instruct you that any amounts which you allow in damages for future pain and suffering of the parents for the loss of their child shall be included in your verdict, and you should not reduce those amounts to present money value. In other words, what Mr. Condon suggested to you the Court will tell you that you cannot do. In other words, if you determine that five dollars an hour is realistic, you say five times two hundred thousand hours, it's a million dollars. You're not to, under the law, consider interest, because there is inflation out there. There is Uncle Sam out there. All of those things should not be considered. And that is what the Court is going to instruct you.

I submit to you, we talked evidence. We talked law to you. Let me say to you, National Car Rental gets paid for assuming this great obligation that they are going to be responsible for. Travelers gets paid, and Allstate gets paid. You know, you don't go up and just get that car from National Car Rental. You pay for it. So all of this great justice that they have come in with, they haven't done us any favor. They come in saying, "Oh, we are really doing them a favor. We are admitting liability." They admitted liability because of one reason, they didn't want you to hear how the accident happened.

I said to you they would throw a couple of slogans at you. Normally what they say is, "You know, that there is a profit in this thing for the parents." Instead, the defendants have called the Williams "profiteers." Normally they say something like, "Money won't bring her back." Instead, the defendants say that the Williams are selling Pamela for a second retirement. Let me tell you, the defendants live under our system of justice, too. The way they survive in this community is because of our system of justice and the system of justice in this community is you don't embarrass people for exercising their rights.

I asked each of you would you agree that Mr. and Mrs. Williams had a right to come into Court and let you decide their case. National Car Rental says the next time anybody comes into court, they better take what we offer or they're going to be called profiteers. They're going to be called—well, you're selling your child for a second retirement. They haven't talked evidence. They haven't talked law to you. They talked slogans. I'm surprised that they didn't argue that Pamela would have gone off and married and things like that. In other words, that she would have only been with them two or three more years. But, if you follow that argument to its logical conclusion, that means that a parent would be entitled to more money for the death of a nineteen-day-old infant than they would for a nineteen-year-old fabulous child.

You can understand now why National Car Rental and Travelers and Allstate hired Mr. Condon. He's a master, and as he said back in law school he got those lessons well. Maybe I did make a mistake on what the law was three thousand years ago. I don't know, but I didn't make a mistake on what our trial professor taught us. Mr. Condon and I do remember that story because we were sitting in that trial law class, and here is the professor who had tried many, many thousands of cases. He asked, "You want to be a trial lawyer?" and he was standing up on this podium. He said, "In order to be a trial lawyer you've got to learn just one thing and that's this fish story I'm going to tell you." He said, "If you got the evidence and you got the law in your favor, you act like a creature of the sea called the barracuda, and you go to the meat of the case and stick to it. Don't let them throw you off." But, he said, "Every once in a while you're going to find a case where you can't even put on a witness, there is no evidence in your behalf, and the law is overwhelmingly against you." He said, "Now, that is the trick," he says, "because in that situation you've got to change. You can't be a barracuda. You have got to be this thing called a squid. And when a squid gets in trouble, you know what a squid does? He emits this black ink all over the water; and it muddies up the water, and the squid escapes in the confusion." I submit to you that Mr. Condon was not only a good student when it came to wrongful death law, but I suggest to you that Mr. Condon really learned to apply the story of the squid and that's all he talked to you about, is muddying the water.

There is no question that Mr. and Mrs. Williams have suffered, and there is no question that they are going to continue to suffer. It will run 200,000 hours from the date of this accident to the day she dies, and it will run one 183,960 hours for Mr. Williams. But, you know, it is inconceivable to me that they wouldn't sit here and wouldn't talk to you about this. They tell you that, "it's unreasonable for the Williams to suffer like this. Why, you know, they are profiteers. They want a second retirement for this girl." And that's what they have talked to you about. No, they haven't sat there and discussed the evidence. They haven't discussed the law. They muddied up the water. Don't let them escape in the confusion.

If it is true that Mrs. Williams isn't suffering and that all these people are liars, if that's really true, and if it is true that Mr. Williams is not really having the problems he's having at home and things like that, they would have brought some evidence of it. They didn't bring any evidence of it. They said, "Why didn't he bring in a psychiatrist?" Obviously, well, the lady is not going to a psychiatrist, and I'm not going to send her to a psychiatrist. If I had sent her to a psychiatrist, then Mr. Condon would have jumped up and said "Mr. Levin sent her to a psychiatrist. He's also in this thing profiteering trying to get the second retirement and all that stuff." The evidence came off the witness stand. If they had had any evidence, they would have put it on.

There is no exact standard for determining a value on 200,000 hours of mental pain and suffering or 100,000 hours of mental pain and suffering or 190,000 hours of mental pain and suffering. But, I submit to you that our suggestion of approximately five dollars per hour is realistic. It's just a little bit more than minimum wage. I submit to you that there is no way that you could pay me or Mr. Condon or anybody five dollars for one hour or fifty dollars or a hundred dollars for just one hour of what they suffer. There is another way to look at it. It's not just what would you pay somebody for what they have gone through, but what would they give not to go through it. You can look at it either way. Well, you think that's not really fair, because if Mr. and Mrs. Rockefeller lost their daughter—or their son—they would pay millions to get the child back. So, it really isn't fair. But, there is something that they would give, and I submit to you that if you believe they would give it, that is of value of their suffering. I submit to you that both of these people would give up both of their legs and both of their arms to have Pam back, and I think they would allow themselves to be rolled around for the rest of their life to have their daughter back. What is that worth? In a clear case of liability, a case where they admit liability and somebody lost both arms and both legs, I submit to you that it would be worth well into the millions of dollars.

There is another method you can use and that is another way that when you go in the jury room I want you to think about and talk about. If you were to put two million dollars in front of these "profiteers," these people looking for their second retirement, and say you can have it or Pam would come walking through that door, which would Mr. and Mrs. Williams choose?

I'm about to finish. Justice in this case demands that the scales be balanced. Pam on one side and your verdict on the other side. Equal compensation for what has been taken. When you fill out that verdict form, what you are saying in writing is: we, the jury, find for the plaintiffs. What you're saying to the Williams is that this is what we feel the value of your loss is, and that's what's going to come back on that piece of paper.

Next week you're going to go back to your jobs, back to your homes, and, you know, you have got your happiness and your sadness and all of the things that happen around you, and you're not going to even really think about this again unless you happen to see Mr. or Mrs. Williams on the street. And I submit to you that you will walk up to them and say, "Remember me, I sat on the jury that determined a value on your loss for the loss of Pam. I hope you are doing better, and I hope our verdict showed to you that we understood your loss, and understood that Pam was one in a million."

## Appendix 5
## TRUCKING ACCIDENT–PERSONAL INJURY–
## $4.8 MILLION JURY VERDICT

### Issues Addressed

- Posing rhetorical questions to opposing counsel to demonstrate absurdity of position

- Utilizing current events and analogies in explaining damages

## IN THE CIRCUIT COURT IN AND FOR ESCAMBIA COUNTY
## STATE OF FLORIDA

WILLIAM I. STONE,
    Plaintiff,

vs.                          Case No. 91-2461-CA-01

SACRED HEART HOSPITAL OF    Division "K"
PENSACOLA.
    Defendant.

---

### Summary of Case

Billy Stone was driving a truck for an acetylene tank gas company. Loaded on the back of the truck were several flammable cylinders. Billy was heading south on a two-lane road and stopped behind a Sacred Heart Hospital bus that was turning left into a Masonic Lodge to provide free medical care. There were three passengers on the bus along with the driver. Heading north was a tractor/trailer unit hauling pulpwood logs. As the pulpwood truck driver approached the lodge, the bus driver turned left in front of the truck. The truck driver then swerved to his left to miss the bus and struck Billy's vehicle, causing the

209

logs to land on Billy's vehicle. The flammable cylinders began to burn, and Billy was trapped in the vehicle, feeling the heat of the flames and inhaling the smoke.

Billy was trapped in the vehicle for forty-five minutes as the Jaws of Life extricated him. Billy was then flown by helicopter to a local hospital. Billy's injuries included fractures of both hips and sexual dysfunction. Billy could only maintain an erection by injecting a drug into the base of his penis.

Sacred Heart Hospital contended that the pulpwood truck driver was 100% at fault, claiming he should have been able to stop in his lane and avoid striking any vehicle. The defense expert testified that the truck driver's perception/reaction time should have been one and one-half seconds. Traveling within the speed limit, the truck driver should have been able to stop approximately thirty feet before striking the bus. Sacred Heart Hospital's maximum offer before trial was $350,000. The trial, which occurred in 1993, resulted in a $4.8 million jury verdict. On appeal, however, the Florida First District Court of Appeals ruled that Fred Levin's closing argument resulted in fundamental error, meaning the argument was so highly inflammatory and prejudicial that no jury could overcome its effect, and thus, no objection was required to preserve the defendant's appellate rights. Specifically, the Court cited Mr. Levin's argument that the defense was "ridiculous" and "insulting." The Florida Supreme Court denied review, and the case was remanded for a second trial. The Florida Bar then brought ethics charges against Mr. Levin, claiming that Mr. Levin had violated *Model Rules of Professional Conduct* Rule 3.4(e), which provides that no lawyer shall in trial "state a personal opinion as to the justness of a cause, the credibility of a witness, the culpability of a civil litigant, or the guilt or innocence of an accused." The ethics charges proceeded to trial. The trial judge found Mr. Levin not guilty on all charges, and the acquittal was upheld by the Florida Supreme Court. The case was settled before the second trial.

Excerpts from the closing argument are included below. The purpose of these excerpts is to show the use of current events or analogies in explaining the damages and also the use of rhetorical questions to the opposing counsel.

### *Excerpts of Closing*

I would like to start by making a comment to Billy Stone. I want to tell you it's an honor and a privilege to represent you. The witnesses that came in and testified, even their witnesses, testified as to what a wonderful person you are. I think you are what this country is all about: honor, family, country, love. It's a pleasure to represent you.

Now to get to the trial. In the last several years there have been two events that I can think of in the news that have been so horrendous that we, as the general public, have just shied away from them. One was the *Challenger* when it went down in 1986 with the crew on board. We were able to accept the fact that they died in that crash. But when the time came and they wanted to find the black box, and they wanted to find out whether these people lived during those sixty or so seconds, the government refused to give that information to the families or to the public, because it was just too much. We could accept the death. We could not accept the fact, as far as they were concerned, of *Challenger* coming down for a period of that length of time, knowing what the individuals on board were saying and that the chances were very slim that they were going to survive.

The other incident I'm going to speak about also occurred in Florida and happened last year. It's not a pleasant thing to talk about, but it was a boyfriend and girlfriend together in Tampa, and the ex-husband came in and held them at bay with a gun and then proceeded to cut off the sexual organ of the boyfriend.

In this case, Billy Stone went through basically both similar situations. Billy Stone was trapped in a truck for approximately forty-five minutes. It was burning. He didn't want to burn to death.

Of course, in Tampa the victim went to the hospital. Whatever condition he's in today, he can't be in any worse shape than Billy Stone, who has a permanent sexual dysfunction.

So what I say to you is that Billy Stone went through two of the most horrendous situations any of us could ever imagine. And he was totally innocent; that, everybody is in agreement about. As horrible as we feel about the boyfriend in Tampa, he knew he was taking somewhat of a chance when he was with somebody's ex-wife. As horrible as we feel about the *Challenger* and what happened to those people, they knew that they were endangering themselves. They also stood to get incredible recognition and probably financial reward as a result.

But Billy Stone was simply sitting there. He didn't know he was in danger. If that accident hadn't happened, he would have gone on to work that day. That evening he would have come home and probably played softball or whatever would have occurred. Maybe he had a date. So this totally innocent 35-year-old man, extremely happy young man, had his life destroyed.

In that destruction, two events took place that we don't want to think about, but you've got to, because both of those things are elements of the damages in this case. Both of those things, the forty-five minutes in a burning vehicle and the sexual dysfunction, are part of the damages in this case.

I know you don't like to discuss things like that, but you've got to. The difficult thing is, you wouldn't even want to discuss it with family and friends, and here you're going to have to discuss it in that jury room with strangers.

I think that's what the defendant in this case is banking on, that you could say, "Gee whiz, I don't even want to talk about it." The easy thing to do is try to find some way out and find no liability.

But I submit to Mr. Baker and Ms. Tipton in this case that they would have been a lot better off realizing that you are going to follow your oath, and you're going to follow the law and the evidence in this case and that you are not going to be swayed by the defense expert who says that the pulpwood truck driver drove for a period of nine seconds into a bus blocking the lane, and he just basically did not touch his brakes or attempt to avoid the collision. This expert testimony is just so incredible that it is ridiculous in light of the evidence.

One thing that I do want to point out, when witnesses are at the scene of an accident and they tell the highway patrolman what happened; that's basically as they see it. It's not the most critical thing in the world to them. And then a year later or two years later they come in to give a deposition, and we lawyers are trained to say, "Well, tell me where you were when this happened; tell me where you were when that happened; tell me how much time that was." And people say, "Well, a minute," and all of a sudden that minute is taken and it's blown up and some expert comes in and takes a stopwatch, and pretty soon this is the whole case.

This is what I have tried to avoid in this case. You can't take a little statement out of a deposition: "Where was the truck when this occurred? How much time was it?" It really is not fair to the witness. It's not fair to you, the jury, to wait a year or two years and take that kind of testimony.

They bring in Mr. Wiggins, the defense expert. He has never driven an 18-wheeler in his life except one time in a parking lot. Yet he comes up with this incredible story. He tells you that a truck driver driving an 18-wheeler has the same perception-reaction time as an automobile driver. What Mr. Wiggins is saying is that in his opinion a truck driver should be able to make an avoidance maneuver as quickly in an 18-wheeler as a person can in a small automobile. That is simply not common sense, and Mr. Wiggins has nothing to back that up. He certainly does not have the personal experience of driving an 18-wheeler fully loaded with logs.

On the other hand, we brought in Dave Stopper who has been driving trucks for years and years and years and has worked for the National Transportation Safety Board. He even teaches truck driving. Mr. Stopper says it's ridiculous to think that a truck driver can react as quickly as an automobile driver. A truck driver has too many things he has to think about when driving a tractor-trailer, including jackknifing, including the load shifting, and things of this nature.

Was Mr. Davis, the pulpwood driver, at fault as Sacred Heart Hospital argues? Now, when Mr. Baker stands up here, I want him to answer that question for you. There's a very simple way to answer it. I want Mr. Baker, Sacred Heart's defense attorney, to assume he was in that Sacred Heart Hospital bus on the day of this accident. The driver of the bus came to a stop and began making a left turn in front of Mr. Davis' truck. Now, Mr. Baker at that moment has a choice; let Mr. Davis, the truck operator, drive like he did the morning of that accident and attempt to swerve into the left lane and try to avoid the bus, or he can do as Mr. Wiggins said and try to slam on his brakes in order to avoid the bus, which, as far as Mr. Davis knew, could have been loaded with children. If Mr. Baker was on that Sacred Heart Bus that day, what does he want Mr. Davis to do—swerve to the left or try to slam on the brakes with a fully loaded 18-wheeler?

The real issue in this case is Billy Stone's pain and suffering in the past and future. The issue is Billy's damages for pain and suffering, disability, physical impairment, disfigurement, mental anguish, inconvenience, and loss of the capacity for the enjoyment of life.

Billy has 43 more years of life in which he will continue to experience his pain. How do we evaluate this? There's no guideline, no yardstick. We could turn to Billy Stone and say, "How much is it worth? He could say, "Gee whiz, I was happy. I wasn't rich, but I was happy. I loved my job. I was active with my son. I had girlfriends. I had lots of friends. I was playing softball, golf, hunting, fishing. I wasn't rich, but I had a very happy life. Now, I'm in constant pain. Sometimes it's horrible. I can't sleep. I don't do anything. I can't play softball. I can't hunt and fish. I can't be real active with my son. Sexually I'm a disaster. I'm depressed. I feel worthless."

I'm sure you would say there's not enough money in the world to pay a person for this. But the law says, and the judge will instruct you shortly, that you must award an amount of money that will fairly and adequately compensate Billy Stone for this injury. You can't just go into that jury room and say there is not enough money in the world and come out with an inadequate or an unfair amount. That wouldn't be right, and that is not the law.

As I stated earlier, I want Mr. Baker to get up here on behalf of Sacred Heart and tell you that if he were a passenger in the bus that day that he would have rather Mr. Davis had tried to stop before hitting the bus than swerve and miss the bus and attempt to avoid Billy Stone. I also ask Mr. Baker to get up here and tell you what he believes Billy's future pain and suffering is worth per hour, for each hour of his life in the future.

I'm going to sit down and look with interest as to how much Mr. Baker thinks per hour this is worth.

Thank you.

### Rebuttal Argument

I'll tell you one thing Mr. Baker was not willing to do. He wasn't willing to do any gambling, was he? I said, "Steve, all you got to do is come up here and look these people in the eye and just tell them I would have been happy to be on that Sacred Heart bus, and I'd have been happy for this man to have perceived and reacted the way Mr. Wiggins said."

He would not tell you that. Nobody would tell you that, because he is not willing to take that gamble. But I'll tell you what, you can bet your bottom dollar that the three people on that Sacred Heart bus were very, very happy Mr. Davis did what he did.

Now the damages. Of all the things Mr. Baker would not do, one thing he would not do is get in that bus, and the other thing he would not do is tell us how much per hour is Billy's future pain and suffering. Why is that?

It's because the pain is every day, every hour. You take 24 hours a day times 365 days per year times 43 years, it comes to over 376,700 hours. Let's just say 375,000 hours. At ten dollars per hour, you're talking about $3,750,000 dollars in future pain and suffering. You talk about the fact that Billy Stone was making $40,000 a year, twenty dollars per hour, for a forty-hour week, and this is the reason that Mr. Baker doesn't want to say anything to you about how much it is. Think about trying to pay someone to go through what Billy Stone will go through for the next 43 years. He can't quit experiencing the pain, as someone can quit a job. He can't say I want one day a month free of pain, to feel like a man, sleep well, go out and play ball, hunt with my son, and just be happy.

I want to close with one comment that I mentioned and then I'll sit down. I mentioned to a friend, "What do you think a case like this is worth?" I explained to him all the things Billy Stone goes through. He called me up last Sunday and he said, "Don't ever, ever tell me about another one of your cases." He said, "I had the worst nightmare last night. I dreamed about Billy Stone." He said, "When I woke up, I was in a cold sweat. I dreamed about that fire. I dreamed about the sex problems. I dreamed about the constant pain and the inability to do anything with my son, family, friends." He said, "It was the worst nightmare I can recall. Don't ever tell me about another one of your cases. I don't want to hear about them."

My friend woke up from a nightmare and went on to experience his normal pleasant day. Billy, unfortunately, wakes up every morning realizing that his life is a nightmare.

Thank you.